'This is a timely bringing together of the key factors around technology enhanced learning. As policy makers are finally waking up to the potential for teachers to amplify their impact with technology, Angela McFarlane is rigorous in her approach to the debate. She successfully shows what works and what to look out for, and leads us to how the latest thinking can really transform teaching.'

Lord Jim Knight, Visiting Professor, London Knowledge Lab, UK

'Angela's book provides a fresh take on the core issues facing researchers and educators when integrating technology into the curriculum. She argues strongly that support for children's learning with technologies must go beyond an "if you build it they will learn" mentality. Her ideas for supporting learning with technologies have practical implications for parents and schools as well as important findings for academics and policy makers in designing for learning.'

Professor Danaë Stanton Fraser, Department of Psychology, University of Bath, UK

Authentic Learning for the Digital Generation

Why should we use technology to support learning?
Where does the responsibility lie to prepare young people to be active and successful cybercitizens?
Can we go on confiscating pupils' smartphones indefinitely?

Authentic Learning for the Digital Generation is a vital examination of young people's use of personal devices, online creative communities and digital gaming. It calls into question the idea of the 'digital native' and shows clearly that the majority of young users need help and support in order to benefit from the rich learning potential of personal, mobile and online technology use.

Written by a leading authority on the role of digital technologies in education, it looks in detail at the practice and implications of learning using personal devices, collaborative online spaces, learning platforms, user-generated content and digital games. In particular, approaches to solving problems, building knowledge, manipulating data and creating texts are examined. It offers clear strategies, a vision for what effects on learning we might reasonably expect when children are given access to different types of technology, and explores the challenges of managing these practices in school and at home.

Authentic Learning for the Digital Generation offers careful analysis at a time when there is much discussion about young people emerging from school unprepared for the world of work and often struggling to manage their personal relationships as they are exposed to strong content and harsh criticism online. It considers what we know of childhood experience in a digital world and offers ways in which schools and teachers can embrace the opportunity presented by ubiquitous ownership of connected, digital devices to enrich and deepen learning. The insights offered may also help parents to understand something of the digital life of their children.

Angela McFarlane has designed and directed a number of highly successful educational research and development projects over a 25-year period. Her development projects have resulted in a range of commercially successful products and reached schools across the world, with impact on learning documented through independent evaluation. She has been an adviser to governments in Europe, South America and South East Asia and the OECD and holds visiting chairs at King's College, London and the University of Bath, UK. Angela is Chief Executive and Registrar of the College of Teachers.

Authentic Learning for the Digital Generation

Realising the potential of technology in the classroom

Angela McFarlane

Routledge
Taylor & Francis Group

LONDON AND NEW YORK

First published 2015
by Routledge
2 Park Square, Milton Park, Abingdon, Oxon OX14 4RN

and by Routledge
711 Third Avenue, New York, NY 10017

Routledge is an imprint of the Taylor & Francis Group, an informa business

British Library Cataloguing in Publication Data
A catalogue record for this book is available from the British Library

Library of Congress Cataloging in Publication Data

ISBN: 978–1–138–01410–7 (hbk)
ISBN: 978–1–138–01411–4 (pbk)
ISBN: 978–1–315–79480–8 (ebk)

Typeset in Sabon
by Swales & Willis, Exeter, Devon

Printed and bound in Great Britain by
TJ International Ltd, Padstow, Cornwall

Contents

Preface

Four decades on from the first computers for schools initiatives, it seems remarkable that there is still a policy debate as to the exact role for digital devices in schools. Meanwhile, the world has moved swiftly. The worlds of work and leisure are now so entwined with that of information and communications technologies (ICTs) that their use is barely worthy of remark. Even watching television, the developed world's main leisure activity, has become an online phenomenon, often accompanied by a 'second screen' as the viewer sends messages to friends and the broadcaster in response to the programme. Knowing a fact from memory may be no more impressive than being able to find it quickly via a search engine. Friends and family are constantly a click away. It is not simply that the preparation for entry into the workforce needs re-thinking, preparation to inhabit the day-to-day world of school-age learners also needs some adjustment. Children experience touchscreens before they can talk, if only through playing with their mother's phone to keep them quiet. Our phones have become the repository for contacts, photographs, and our first choice for communications and, increasingly, commercial transactions.

There is a false premise that because children have been born into a world of ubiquitous computing they are naturally able to master digital technologies. While they may be free of preconceptions as to how difficult or strange using such tools may be, left to their own devices their use tends mainly to the banal and trivial. This book looks at the impact of near-universal device ownership, access to collaborative online spaces, sharing of creative output online and the importance of collaborative problem solving in a connected digital world. These are the experiences of the digital native that have relevance and therefore authenticity for them. They are part of their social lives at school and will be part of their professional lives thereafter. Currently schools are not preparing learners adequately to function at their full capacity in this digital world. This book looks at why that might be and why it is vitally important we re-think what it means to be well-educated in a knowledge society. It also offers some suggestions as to how school practice might meet this challenge. This book is for anyone interested in education of school-age children and young people, and particularly those teachers, managers and policy makers who ultimately determine what we recognise as educational success.

Acknowledgements

I would like to thank the hundreds of learners and teachers who have welcomed me into their classrooms over the last three decades and who have proved an inexhaustible source of inspiration for this book. I could not have begun to make sense of what I have seen over the years without the help of excellent researchers who have worked with me on successive projects. Many thanks to Ketta Williams, Nel Roche, Fern Faux, Helen Thornham, Pat Triggs, Marie Joubert Gibbs and Wan Ching Yee. I have benefited from the many conversations I have had with doctoral and master's students I have worked with over the years, as well as friends and colleagues across the world. Special thanks go to Miguel Nussbaum. And finally to Bryan Berry, who lives the day-to-day reality of bringing first-rate education to young people and who makes sure that I stay grounded.

Thanks to the following for permission to use images:

- Amantia Design for the screenshot in Chapter 7;
- Kurt Squire for the figure in Chapter 7;
- Charles Crook for re-assembling the figure in Chapter 1 so I could use it here.

List of abbreviations

APU	Assessment of Performance Unit
ATL	Association of Teachers and Lecturers
BBC	British Broadcasting Company
BEEP	BioEthics Education Project
BESA	British Education Suppliers Association
BYOD	Bring Your Own Device
CEOP	Child Exploitation and Online Protection
CPD	continuing professional development
CSCL	computer-supported collaborative learning
GOM	Game Object Model
ICT	information and communications technology
IT	information technology
LPP	legitimate peripheral participation
MIS	management information system
MIT	Massachusetts Institute of Technology
MOOC	massive open online course
OECD	Organization for Economic Cooperation and Development
OLPC	One Laptop Per Child
PISA	Programme for International Student Assessment
QCA	Qualifications and Curriculum Agency
RSE	relationships and sex education
SRE	sex and relationships education
SWGfL	South West Grid for Learning
TEEM	Teachers Evaluating Educational Multimedia
UGC	user-generated content
UKCCIS	United Kingdom Council for Child Internet Safety
VLE	virtual learning environment

Introduction

The generation born since 2000 has experienced childhood in a very different world from that of their parents and teachers. This 'digital generation' are growing up, live and will work in a world where digital technologies are truly ubiquitous. Much of the early promise of digital technologies has begun to emerge in the home and workplace, although the majority of schools are still relatively untouched. These technologies are changing the way we communicate, create and share knowledge, consume information, present ourselves to our immediate circle and the wider world, shop and play. The impact on our leisure choices is already profound and time spent in front of screens has increased to the point where it has been proposed as a factor in increasing levels of child obesity. Time online is overtaking time watching TV. Given all these changes, a question arises as to whether the education children and young people experience in formal schooling is an adequate preparation for economic and social adult life (McFarlane, 2006). Further, to what extent does that education have personal relevance to the children and young people as they go through the system? Is the learning they are expected to do, and on which their educational success will be measured, in any way authentic?

The starting point for this book was a re-examination of a volume I edited entitled *IT and Authentic Learning* (McFarlane, 1997). I assumed when I started that the majority of the content in the original book would no longer be relevant to education nearly 20 years later; times had changed, software evolved, devices are cheaper and more powerful. But on re-reading the book and various research project reports I and others have worked on in the intervening years, I was surprised to discover how little the fundamentals have changed. There is often an assumption that the speed of development of the technology itself is so rapid – nothing is expected to last more than two years – that the learning from research that is not contemporary is no longer relevant. In reality this is simply not the case. Not only does the research remain relevant but also some of the practice remains unchanged and aspects of policy look remarkably familiar. In the time I have been working on this new volume I have been in conversation with representatives from a range of the leading global technology companies who provide goods and services to homes and businesses and also have an interest in education. I have been privy to conversations regarding education policy development between these companies and senior government representatives. I have talked to a selection of those in schools as managers, teachers and learners and those who work to support their use of digital technology. My research has encompassed the UK and other Organization for Economic Cooperation and Development (OECD) members, particularly the US. The truth is that the reality of technology access and use in schools has changed little for the majority, and the questions asked regarding the role of technology in schools at the policy level remain remarkably similar even though the world of personal technology use beyond school is almost unrecognisable.

Devices themselves, although very different in many ways from those of the millennium, and access to the services needed to support their use such as fast broadband remain expensive for schools. As consumer prices have fallen, home provision outshines that in school for the vast majority, as it did for the minority with home access in the past. Students who are allowed to use devices in school get better internet connectivity through their phones than through the school wi-fi. The ratios of students to computers in schools have in effect worsened as the percentage of devices over five years old has increased. The model of one-to-one computing, piloted and evaluated for over 20 years, remains the preserve of the special project or innovative school. Presumably since home access generally has grown across the board, teachers do have better access to technology than they once did at home if not in the workplace. Government no longer sees a need to subsidise portable device ownership for teachers as they did at the turn of the twenty-first century.

It is a brave commentator who predicts the pace of change in relation to technology adoption in education as the record is littered with overly optimistic projections. Each new technology, from waxed cylinders used for sound recording in 1894 onwards has been hailed as *the* answer to schooling, replacing costly teachers and 'delivering' learning directly to pupils cheaply and efficiently (Uzanne, 1894). Each technology has in turn been absorbed into schools to a greater or lesser extent, but none of the predictions of revolution have come to pass. However, figures from market research suggest that we may finally be on the verge of a sea change at least in terms of access to digital devices. The combination of phone and powerful computing and display devices is the foundation of a global explosion in personal ownership of connected devices across the developed world with some countries seeing huge increases in a short time; 2010–12 seems to have been a tipping point. Pricing models for hardware and connectivity have made purchase and use affordable or at least manageable, enabling ownership to be extended to school-age students. In the case of tablet devices, the penetration extends to younger children where touchscreen technology has had a particular impact. In many countries, a majority of the school population has access to a device at home that they could potentially take to school. At this point, most schools are reluctant to exploit this resource by allowing pupils to bring devices to school, although many are investing in some portable devices for use within school. The reasons for this reluctance are not simply those of cost, or cost control. They are related to control of a different sort but they are also related to the models of what it means to learn and the nature of proof used to acknowledge progress in the development of knowledge or skills.

It seems that at the heart of the question of what an appropriate pedagogy using digital technology looks like is, unsurprisingly, a philosophical question of what it means to know, or a wider social question of what we expect from an 'education'. In a testing dominated policy culture, where the results of tests are used to police the accountability and performance of schools and individual teachers, the forms of learning outcomes that are amenable to measurement through testing are privileged. There is an inevitable bias that favours those who can recall factual content as declarative knowledge, which is the cheapest and easiest form of learning to assess consistently. Schools that are succeeding in this context vary enormously in their use of technology and it is clear that it is perfectly possible to prepare learners for these assessments with little or no use of technology by the learners as many schools with low technology use prove.

One consequence of the general low level of use of technology in schools is that children and young people are having a range of experiences, many rich and powerful, using digital technologies that are not part of their experience of school. Debates on the role of technology in learning commonly focus on the view that as a result of their experience out of school, learners are bored by school, have shortened attention spans, a tendency to use a version of written language developed for short messaging services and are overly inclined to copy and paste information uncritically. There are also concerns about the exposure online to inappropriate content and behaviour such as cyberbullying. Despite widespread unrest, currently we lack a shared view of the implications of these changes for the role of schools, but surely there is a need for schools to address these issues and help to prepare learners to be thoughtful and effective users of technology?

In this book I discuss what we know of the life of the digital generation and the growing disconnect between experiences in and out of school. I look at the promise and peril of personal device use with constant connectivity, the need for an induction into socially acceptable behaviours online as well as offline, the increasing gap between what students learn at school and what they need to be employed afterwards. Referencing key national studies and international comparative research, I look at the evolving experience of young people as they both assimilate digital technology into their lives and progress through formal education. I look at some of the particular affordances of digital technology that can be brought to bear to support learning: feedback, mutability, communication, reach. Drawing on a range of longitudinal studies I have led, I look at what we have learned about sustained use of one-to-one devices and powerful online communities and ask what the implications of each are for mainstream schooling. Much of this research was originally published in reports for the then UK government body for educational technology, but when this was closed its web-based content was dispersed and became difficult to locate. This book brings a little of it back into the public domain. I also reach back to draw on some early research into the relationship between computer use and learning, citing sources I believe have enduring relevance and validity and should not be lost. The look of the device, the user interface, the speed may change but some fundamentals remain relevant. The importance of access and duration, the need to shape the task and the need to ground the screen-based learning in a wider context all remain pertinent.

This book will not tell you how technology should be used in the classroom, at least not at the level of the lesson plan, but it does make an argument as to why it should be used, critically and thoughtfully. If schools do not take responsibility for educating young people to be good citizens online as they do offline, who will take that role? Many parents are unable or unwilling to intervene as their children are immersed in a set of experiences that are possibly alien to them and certainly played no part in their own childhoods. At the same time, powerful interests are all too ready and willing to exploit the access these technologies give them to the young and impressionable. The constant contact they have with each other is also a mixed blessing. On a happier note, digital technologies and access to information and people beyond school have enormous potential to support effective learning. They can be used to empower every individual with the tools to create knowledge that is at the same time personal to them, socially constructed and relevant to the wider world. It is the combination of empowerment as a user of technology and a creator of deep, personally relevant knowledge that brings authenticity to education and prepares school students to live happy and fulfilling lives in the world they inhabit beyond school.

Clearly this book concentrates on the use of technology to support learning, both in and out of school. In reading it, the impression is of a context where the machine-based interaction is the sole experience of learning. It is important to note, however, that this is far from the vision I would wish to promote. It is important to use technology and particularly to teach children and young people to use it well, but when in school the most important resources any learner has access to are skilled teachers and their fellow learners. Face-to-face interactions are at a premium in the relatively few hours a year they spend in class. While that experience can be supported, enhanced and extended through meaningful technology-mediated experience, it is really important that students also get to interact with each other and the real world. The most dispiriting use of computers in school I have ever seen was a lesson where the class spent the whole lesson working through exercises on an excellent revision website. Certainly this was a worthwhile part of exam preparation but one that could and should have been done in the time they were not with a qualified teacher or, arguably, the rest of the class. As well as knowing why and when to use technology, it is just as important to know when to turn the machines off and talk.

References

McFarlane, A.E. (ed.) (1997) *IT and Authentic Learning – Realising the Potential of Computers in the Primary Classroom.* London: Routledge.

McFarlane, A.E. (2006) ICT and the curriculum canon: responding to and exploring 'alternative knowledge', in Moore, A. *Schooling Society and Curriculum.* London: Routledge (pp. 130–42).

Uzanne, O. (1894) The end of books. *Scribner's Magazine Illustrated*, 16 (July–December), pp. 221–31.

Chapter 1

The digital learning landscape

Where are we now?

The long-anticipated era of ubiquitous computing has finally arrived. Predicted, lauded and longed for, the day when every learner can have a powerful computing device in their hand is here, but the reality does not look exactly like the vision set out from the early 1970s when personal computers first appeared. That the device is an evolution of the phone, and designed first to communicate then to consume content and services, is not what educational technologists were imagining in the era of the 'teaching machine'. The 'smartphone' is a remarkable amalgam of the phone, computer, camera and television, which is not quite like any of them, and yet is more than all four together. It is, finally, cheap enough, and with service plans that are manageable enough, that few think twice before acquiring them for, or at least passing them on to, their children, although the precise age at which this is appropriate is disputed.

The smartphone sits at one end of a spectrum of multifunctional, connected devices designed to be personal to one user and carried with them wherever they choose to take them. At the other end of the mobile spectrum is the notebook or laptop computer, which has all the functions of a desktop computer in a more compact form. Along the spectrum sits a range of devices with a mixture of attributes of the two ends and some of their own. Somewhere in the middle sit devices with touchscreens, larger than phones and usually with a different operating system to personal computers, broadly these are described as 'tablets'. Together these are the mobile devices that have changed the way society uses digital technologies, and arguably the fabric of society itself, through the impact on how we communicate with and thus relate to each other. These devices and the networks they support are changing the way we learn and also carry the potential to change the way we teach (McFarlane, 2003, 2010).

School models of technology adoption tend to lag behind those in wider society in developed countries. For the most part learners have better access to technology at home than in school. Schools in many OECD countries installed computer rooms with fixed machines attached to wired networks in the 1980s and 1990s. In most schools these remain and continue to have a use where large and complex software applications are used and/or internet access requires bandwidth that wireless technology cannot support. These are increasingly supplemented with sets of mobile devices. Given the limitations of the installed base in schools it seems logical that schools would look to a mixed economy where they provide the specialist applications and peripherals, and support the few who do not have their own devices, but that the norm is for learners to bring and use their own personal, mobile devices to support their learning.

However, another thing that educational technologists did not predict was that schools would be quite so hostile to these personal devices. And why should that be so? There can be no doubt that connectivity – and these devices are built to be constantly connected – is highly disruptive. For one thing it brings the outside world into school in an unprecedented way. Even 10 years ago the idea that parent and child would be able to communicate at any given point in the school (and work) day was novel. Now it is commonplace to have a colleague answer a mobile in a work context because it is their child calling or texting. A powerful, personal device is empowering and can be both hypnotic and somewhat addictive (as in the compulsive checking of email and social media). You are in constant possession of it and it connects you to the world; the norm is to have it switched on at all times. Being active on your social media account, and receptive to the posts others make, is a 24/7 expectation. You are always available to those you know in this world, and if you do not protect your contact information or do not understand or use security settings judiciously, to everyone else as well. Not all of the consequences of this widespread and constant connectivity are positive; cyberbullying is rampant and a majority of teenage girls have been exposed unwillingly to online porn (Horvath et al., 2013).

In the classroom, whether it is using a search engine to find additional information relevant to the lesson, or a camera to capture and then share an image of a difficult moment in classroom management, there is potential to use these devices for purposes that challenge the teacher's authority and disrupt the lesson even when that use is a legitimate extension to the individual's own learning. Certainly this potential is enough to see many schools place a blanket ban on mobile device use in school, and in some cases on bringing one onto the premises. It even sees schools that provide students with personal devices setting up a policy and written agreement that curtails use of them in school to only that clearly sanctioned by a teacher. So it seems there is an uneasy relationship between school and personal technology that at worst sees the school as somewhat beleaguered by an onslaught of technology-wielding children.

This is both sad and troubling. Sad because when used well, digital technologies do have the potential to enrich and transform our lives and are doing so in many spheres. Troubling because unless adults embrace the use of these technologies by the young, and guide and steward their use of them, we leave them 'adrift on a sea of meaning' (Sanger, 1997) and that sea is a far more stormy one than any of us could perhaps have imagined in the calmer days when Sanger was worrying about access to TV, video and microcomputers. Moreover, where schools fully understand the power of digital technology to support learning and develop a culture and practice that can harness that power, learners benefit from a powerful personalised experience that helps prepare them for an economically and socially rewarding adult life.

Understanding the power of digital technology to support learning

It is too easy to become either mesmerised or blasé when confronted with the myriad functions of a twenty-first-century mobile device. In place of a range of devices that did one thing and only one thing, we now have in our pockets or bags a device that does something more with each iteration. At the time of writing the latest feature being used to sell hardware and services is streaming live television to your phone or tablet. You can watch wherever you are (or to be precise wherever you have adequate wireless or phone network coverage) and you can even join in. Broadcast media regularly request audience members to send them messages through a variety of instant channels, which they then edit and use in the broadcast within minutes. Indeed it is not even necessary to contact them directly. Anyone can broadcast text and images through a microblog; news media outlets constantly scan the cybersphere for breaking stories. If you witness an incident you can be on the next TV news telling your version and available on their website, possibly in perpetuity. Citizen journalism is all the rage.

Given this dazzling potential for every individual to access and create powerful content it is perhaps unsurprising that we may feel the skills and knowledge we have from a more traditional setting no longer have any relevance. Indeed there are many techno-romantics only too ready to insist this is the case and to claim that the best option is to leave the young to teach themselves using technology and for teachers especially to get out of the way (Prensky, 2001, 2012). This then fuels a backlash and feeds into policies that call for a 'back to basics' approach and regular testing of traditional skills and knowledge to hold the school system accountable for improvements in education standards. This dichotomy is unhelpful when it comes to reasoned debate about the shape and nature of a desirable school curriculum or what the role of technology in that curriculum should be. In reality much that we know about learning, communicating, creating knowledge and sharing it, remains valid in the face of connected digital technologies. Recognising this and adapting effective practice to new contexts is at the heart of understanding how digital technologies can best support effective teaching and meaningful, authentic learning. It also helps to have a clearly articulated view of what authentic learning is and what the outcomes of successful learning will look like. The ability to access text with confidence remains a pre-requisite of digital literacy, and it remains pretty handy to be numerate even if only to understand your energy and tax bills!

As well as opportunities there are new challenges in educating learners who are constantly connected. With powerful access to one another through social media, and the opportunity for anonymity, it is more important that ever to instil a strong ethical and moral sense in the young. Without respect for one another as fellow human spirits it seems too many of us are drawn to behaviours that would be unthinkable in a face-to-face context and embrace anonymity to cover our worst excesses. It seems Dostoyevsky was right when he suggested that we are drawn to the dark side when we think we can get away with it.

The challenge for schools

After billions of pounds of investment, endless evaluation and reams of policy documents it seems that the precise role of technology in schools remains unclear. A school achieving outstanding results in terms of test scores may or may not be using digital technology at the heart of its curriculum and culture. After more than 40 years of debate on what effective technology supported learning and pedagogy should be there are still no simple and clear answers in this complex and nuanced debate. What is clear is that there remains a substantial gap between what effective technology-supported learning and pedagogy could be and what happens in the majority of schools. The digital landscape confronting teachers, teacher educators, policy makers, designers and those who would sell products and services to education is something of a minefield, or as Fullan and Donnelly (2013) call it, a swamp.

Fullan and Donnelly identify three main areas of failure of technology programmes to support innovation in schools beyond those involved in intensive projects: pedagogy, system change and technology. Having well-designed, robust technology that is a delight to use is essential and all too often this is not the case in schools where there may be underinvestment in the infrastructure, technical support and training. It is also useful to have a theoretical framework against which to evaluate how that technology use might then impact on learning and therefore the fit with the desired pedagogical models. One place to start is to look at what digital devices do best and consider how that functionality might support teaching and learning.

What do digital devices do best?

Responding to the user

There is no doubt that at the heart of the addictive nature of digital devices is that when you interact with them, you get feedback. You touch, speak to, gesture or shake the device and something happens. First attempts may be somewhat random, but persistence is usually rewarded and gradually you work out how to do a few basic things. This is the basis for the claim that these devices have an intuitive design – you can work out how to make it work, at least at entry level. Moreover having done so there is some consistency across devices and applications so that initial learning can be useful more widely. And the reason you can do this is that your trial and error learning is not blind, but supported by responses, visual, audio or haptic, designed to prompt and guide you and serve as a reminder when you next come to the device. Moreover, the major providers have converged on a few basic similarities in how the devices all work (buttons, menus, 'windows', icons and so on) so that once you have mastered one, you can quickly make a start on the next. Indeed, so similar are these interfaces that legal battles for claimed infringements of copyright are common.

The use of tablets, with their touchscreens, by very young children is a recent and growing phenomenon. The *Zero to Eight* report (Rideout, 2013) suggests half the children in that age group in the US have experience of using one. Certainly the touchscreen interface is proving very easy for young children to use and can support them to carry out activities they might struggle with in other contexts. Studies of the effects of giving very young children aids to increase the control of their actions, for example by enhancing their motor skills, are not new and research is ongoing into the effects of tablet use. As yet there are no conclusive results, and as always there are enthusiasts and those with reservations. That said there are pre-schools that are making very effective use of tablets as part of a varied experience that still incorporates structured and unstructured play in real-world multi-sensory contexts such as the a trip to the park or an afternoon of finger painting!

Of course good use of feedback to support novices goes way beyond simply learning to operate the device itself. The principle of feedback as support for the user to learn to use a device, service or application is inherent to the technology interface. Modern operating systems offer a user experience that de facto supports learning. This aspect of device and software design has been widely exploited to create experiences that can help new and novice users in a range of settings, many of which are not thought of first and foremost as designed learning environments. Much maligned not least due to the high profile of those with violent and otherwise pornographic content and the claimed addictive nature of the play experience, computer games in fact offer excellent examples of interactions designed to help us learn (Gee, 2003) through clues and feedback on our choices and behaviours.

It should be no surprise that digital devices offering users meaningful feedback support efficient learning. The role of feedback to support learning, primarily in the form of formative assessment, is well documented (Black and Wiliam, 1998 and see Association for Achievement and Improvement through Assessment – www.aaia.org.uk). Simple algorithms can be programmed to offer effective formative feedback during a learning task, especially one designed to offer an opportunity for trial and error or practice-based learning. Take for example the simple comparison of two children grappling with a sheet of sums, one with and one without feedback as they go. In the first scenario, each time they give an answer to a problem, they are told whether the answer is correct or not. In the second, they get no response and do not know at the end of the exercise if they have mastered the skill they have been practising, or even made any improvement. Indeed at worst they have simply rehearsed a misconception about addition that they had at the start. Which child is likely to have had the more effective learning experience?

And of course the feedback offered by a well-designed program may not stop at simply marking the answers as you go. It may be that you cannot enter an incorrect answer and must get it right before proceeding, or if you enter more than one or two incorrect answers you are told the right one, and possibly shown how it was achieved. Automated feedback to support closed tasks such as performing arithmetic functions or writing accurate text is widespread both in software designed to support learning and productivity tools such as spreadsheets and word processors. And yet its power is often overlooked or taken for granted as when during the TEEM (Teachers Evaluating Educational Multimedia) project we asked teachers to evaluate the potential of different packages, some of which did not offer feedback and others which offered responses of varying sophistication. Few teachers took account of this variable in their assessments of the products they tested unless they were prompted.

The sophisticated learning packages designed to use feedback to best effect present tasks to the learner in an order determined by both their immediate and historic performance. They also provide reports to the teacher on each pupil's progress. Such systems were widely trialled and used in the 1990s with extensive evaluation and reporting (McFarlane, 1996; Underwood and Brown, 1996). Schools that really embraced such systems used the assessment data they produced to group children working at similar levels and to plan their maths curriculum accordingly. Adjustments could be made on a daily or weekly basis as necessary since a daily 15-minute session on the system was all that each child required to complete exercises and provide assessment data. Large-scale trials showed clear improvements in learning of the subject matter covered when schools were supplied with well-designed products. Children held back by a culture that did not celebrate academic success expressed their liberation when using a system that gave them the privacy to succeed. And yet these systems have never become mainstream, although the use of online mathematics practice software is widespread. Cost was clearly a factor but these systems were and remain controversial with some educators and education commentators (e.g. Stager, 2013). These 'teaching systems', and indeed drill and practice software more broadly, have come to embody the dispute between the factions that argue for a learner-centric model of curriculum designed around access to powerful technology and those preferring a more traditional model. Clearly these instructional systems cannot replace a well-rounded experience of education, or of technology, but it seems that something may be missed if they are excluded entirely as a legitimate part of a rich mix of experiences, provided the cost is proportionate to the benefit. The tensions arise when limited access to technology leads to time 'drilling' becoming the only experience of technology there is in school.

Handling information

Digital devices are extremely good at searching, sorting and displaying information in a wide variety of forms. Connected devices take these features to a whole new level as they can search the effectively infinite repository that is the worldwide web and harness the processing power of other computers to enhance the speed and complexity of computation. Text, numbers, sound, pictures, video and animations can all be stored, manipulated, combined and displayed quickly. These representations can then be shared in an instant, with one or a few selected collaborators or with anyone who wants to access them (an important distinction that has caused widespread embarrassment and more to many!).

Information found when learners search on the web might have been provided by a recognised authority: a museum, broadcaster, world-leading artist or scientist, or by a random individual with an interest and an opinion. It could be as diverse as the original collected papers of Charles Darwin, published to celebrate his bicentenary in 2009 by Cambridge University, the full collection of a major gallery or museum (The National Gallery in London was one of the first to digitise and publish its collection, the majority of which is not on public display at any one time), a wiki entry on a well-known person made by a detractor, a story written by a child in a far-away country about their life or the term's weather data collected in your school as part of a national project. The advantage of a device that can access all this rich and varied information is that it can be searched and selected according to reliability, need and interest as and when a task requires. Links can be made, patterns explored, connections analysed. Provenance can be investigated, sources can be verified and cross-referenced. Items can be edited and used to create a personal account. If copyright and citation are understood, this version can then be shared for comment and feedback.

How powerful access to such rich and varied information and information handling tools is in supporting learning depends on the understanding of the user of what they are seeing and hearing. The ability to distinguish between authoritative and other sources is not well developed in children who can be overly influenced by production values and overly trusting of search engines (McFarlane and Roche, 2003). Any source, no matter how extensive, will have been selected by someone – and that includes the selection of sources returned by a search using a web search engine. Things will have been left out, or added, based on criteria that may or may not be explicit. The author(s) may have an agenda that means that the source is heavily biased, unrepresentative or just plain wrong. Value judgements will have been made. Any reader of the results must be aware of the need to establish the provenance of any source they use, and preferably use more than one source to check any information they want to use. Luckily, this can be done quickly and easily once you know how, but it does mean more than simply reading the first few results you get from a single search engine. Inexperienced users can be overly influenced by the appearance of web source, or naive as to the quality of information available on the internet, and lessons in critical use of sources should be a standard part of the curriculum from an early age.

The ability of a digital device to handle information does not depend solely on a connection to the internet or very large data sets, and neither does its power as a learning tool. The ability to generate a text on a screen, whether it is composed of words, pictures, numbers, video, animation or a selection of any of these, offers three powerful advantages over paper-based media.

First, there is the power to edit and revise. The content created can be changed and reworked as your thoughts form and develop and you gather more information. Drafting and editing become a natural part of the process of authoring a text, even when this is done against the clock. It is a very different activity to writing on paper, or taking photographs or shooting film, which are primarily linear processes. No matter how many times you edit, add to and correct a digital text, the appearance of the finished product is not compromised. There is no need to re-write the whole thing to create a good copy. It is easy to keep versions to show how the work has developed.

Second, it is easy to share copies. This causes concern for teachers as they worry about plagiarism and cheating, however the positive side of this facility is that work can be commented on by the teacher or fellow learners, and re-edited to take account of that feedback quickly and easily.

Finally, the texts learners create can incorporate content from a range of sources. Again this raises concerns, but it is never too early to learn about appropriate citation and making sure you have permission to use other people's content. The end result can be a far richer record of the content covered, and creating these texts offers learners the chance to engage with powerful ideas using a range of sources to make comparisons, search for links and analyse sources. This can only be achieved when the learners have adequate access to devices powerful enough to support content creation by the user, and space to store their work.

Collaboration

The power of computer use to support collaborative learning is such that it has become an area of education research with its own conferences and journal. It is known as CSCL – computer-supported collaborative learning. This support can take many forms from software packages that require input from more than one user to online environments with content repositories, discussion boards and tools that support multiple authors working on the same document. At the heart of all this is the requirement for interaction between learners as part of the learning task.

The model of learning here is social and assumes both that we learn better when we learn together and that digital systems that combine the elements of feedback and connectivity can support such models in a variety of ways (Crook, 1994; Zurita and Nussbaum, 2007; Dillenbourg and Fischer, 2007). These ideas are expanded upon and explored throughout this volume.

Ideally learners should be able to access systems offering these features in and out of school, to share versions of work with teachers, family members and selected fellow learners, and to maintain access to their work over time. Only then can the affordances of powerful digital devices to support learning be fully exploited.

Audience and motivation

When work is digital, it can be shared. When a digital device is on a network, content can be shared over that network whether that is with a closed, school community, a personal network of friends and family or anyone who can access the internet. The potential audience for a learner's school work has moved from being the teacher (and often not even that) to include a parent or carer, a class-mate or friend in another school, the whole class, the whole school, 'anyone who knows me' or just anyone. Developing an understanding of the reach and impact of any form of publishing is an essential element of digital literacy. First and foremost, care must be taken to ensure that the potential audience is at the level the learner intended and that they understand how persistent content is likely to be once shared.

As well as having access to an audience who can encourage and critique your work, in a networked environment a learner can also see and comment on other people's work. It is important to learn how to interact with other people online and this interaction can be a source of inspiration and exemplification. It goes beyond having the best essay read out in class. Students are exposed to a range of work and encouraged to view it critically – what is good here and why, what could be better, can this inform your own approach to the topic? Once the sharing of work can be used competently, it opens up the possibility of motivating students by giving them a purpose to their work, and a satisfaction that goes beyond sim-ply doing as they are asked by a teacher or getting a good mark to show a parent, important though both of these remain.

Getting your hands on a digital device

The potential power of digital technologies lies in the personal use of devices to access and create content as well as connecting to other learners as and when appropriate. This then begs the question of how realistic it is to assume that chil-dren and young people have such access at school or at home. Wherever you are, the picture will be remarkably patchy. Inevitably these technologies remain costly and access will be related to overall economic status of a country, region and household. In the UK in 2012, 93 per cent of all households with children owned a computer, and 89 per cent had access to the internet via a computer. Over 60 per cent of children living in the poorest two deciles of households had access to the internet (Office for National Statistics, 2012). That still means 756,000 school-age children could not go online from a computer at home, and 653,000 could not access a computer. These are highly likely to be the same children at risk of under-performing.

Quality of access to ICT in school remains highly variable, with a number of issues affecting the quality of the learners' experience. Technology moves fast and devices take a lot of wear and tear in schools. Devices and software need to be updated every three to four years. Connectivity is also an issue. Wireless networks to support many hundreds of users accessing high-quality content simultaneously are rare outside educational settings and most schools in the UK do not have sufficient bandwidth on fixed or wireless networks to support enough users accessing rich media simultaneously. Neither do they have enough wireless-enabled devices. Often a student can perform a web search on their phone using the network coverage faster than they can on a fixed school connection. In the US the need for every individual to have an internet-capable device and access to sufficient wireless bandwidth at home and school is recognised in the US Department of Education, Office of Educational Technology's report *Transforming American Education: Learning Powered by Technology* (2010), and it is also an aspiration of the Singapore ICT Masterplan 3 (2011).

The UK is widely regarded as a leader in the provision of ICT infrastructure in publicly funded schools. Yet an industry survey in the UK in 2012 found that primary schools have just 49 computers per school on average, of which only 20 are portable devices (41 per cent) such as laptops or tablets. Each computer is shared between just under seven pupils and 27 per cent of all computers are over five years old. In comparison, secondary schools have 352 computers per school on average of which 97 are portable (28 per cent). Each computer is shared by 4.2 pupils but 24 per cent of all computers are over five years old (BESA, 2013). Average pupil to computer ratios have not materially changed since 2008 in either primary or secondary schools, so the percentage increase in old machines means that individual access to an effective computer is deteriorating. This is a long way from the vision of one device per learner.

Teacher access is more promising with access to a computer in the classroom approaching 100 per cent and data-projection devices – usually interactive whiteboards – being widespread. However, where this is the main configuration it does tend to a teacher-dominated use of technology with presentation software being the most widespread application and pupil use in class being limited to showing slides they have prepared at home or in the computer suite.

As with almost any aspect of schooling, it is easy but dangerous to make sweeping generalisations and averages hide a wide range of provision. The statistics may help us to see percentages of teachers and learners who have physical access to technology but this is far from the whole picture. How those technologies are used is key to their role in supporting teaching and learning, and there is a very wide range of practice in play.

What to do with technology once you have it?

There is a long history of providing digital technologies to schools and looking for impact through improvements in standardised test scores. Evidence of success measured in this way is scarce and, where it does exist, it is restricted to small-scale projects with high levels of technology provision and/or staffing that are not sustainable in the long term and certainly not scalable to whole-school systems. And yet the pervasive nature of digital-technology adoption in industry, commerce and wider society has driven a broad consensus that students should be using technology in schools, if only to prepare them to be economically and socially active and effective in the world of work. Those who advocate widespread adoption of technology also argue for an accompanying change in the approach to learning and teaching that can be summarised as moving from a culture where the teacher leads to one where the learner leads and takes responsibility for their learning. This, in turn, calls for an emphasis on development of the skills needed to be an effective learner and knowledge builder to prepare for a world where new information bombards us 24/7 and change is a constant.

Schools are thus left in a difficult position. If they invest in digital technology, which remains relatively expensive when the size of school budgets are considered, even in wealthy countries, they need to see a tangible return. The most easily evidenced impact is test scores – so how to use the technology to support learning for examinations? And at the same time how to bring in the learning to learn using technology elements – remembering that in an average school any one student will have access to a device for about 15 per cent of the time in secondary and less in primary?

In order to see how schools are responding to this dilemma, an evaluation project in the UK looked in detail at 85 classrooms in schools where use of ICT was well established (Crook et al., 2010). The authors concluded that:

- *ICT makes possible new forms of classroom practice.* This is apparent in three particular respects: (1) the reconfiguration of space such that new patterns of mobility, flexible working and activity management can occur; (2) new ways in which class activities can be triggered, orchestrated and monitored; (3) new experiences associated with the virtualisation of established and routine practices – such as using multiple documents in parallel or manipulating spatial representations.

- *ICT creates the possibility of a wide variety of learning practices.* Overarching this variety are three central activities that are significantly enriched by the increasingly ubiquitous availability of technologies: (1) exposition that is animated by the opportunity to invoke rich shared images, video and plans; (2) independent research that is extended by the availability of internet search opportunities; and (3) construction that is made possible by ready-to-hand ICT-based tools.

It seems that these schools are combining elements of the possible models of computer use and achieving a spread of pedagogic approaches.

Since the earliest large-scale study of impact of digital technology on learning in the UK in 1993 (Watson, 1993), three factors have been recognised as determining the extent to which impact on teaching and learning is likely to be achieved: the physical access to devices (numbers and distribution); the knowledge of the teachers about the use of those technologies; and the importance of digital technologies to the leadership of the school. It seems these remained key nearly 20 years later in the Crook et al. (2010) work where they identified redefining learning spaces (again related to numbers and distribution of equipment), multi-faceted staff development and evolving vision and leadership as common themes key to the effective use of ICT in schools. The use of space in different ways in order to facilitate different modes of working and therefore different distributions of devices is particularly interesting (see Figure 1.1).

Flexibility is important here as both furniture and computers can be arranged and re-arranged to suit the task in hand. This is very different from the fixed-bench model in traditional ICT suites, workshops or science rooms.

Clearly what emerges is that there is no one right answer to the question of how to use technology effectively and as a result hybrid models are emerging. In the circular relationship between technology, pedagogy and system change (Fullan and Donnelly, 2013), it seems to me that the starting point must be with the pedagogy. The most important questions surely are what do we want the learners to know and be able to do at the end of a learning activity and how will that be demonstrated? Unless these are clearly articulated and ideally shared with the learners, how will success ever be meaningfully judged? The same questions apply, albeit at a different scale, for a teacher planning a lesson or course, to a policy maker writing curriculum legislation, a parent choosing a school or a journalist writing a critique of the latest examination results. In the OECD countries currently we are in a state of flux – not satisfied with the results we are getting (not enough or too many students getting high grades, too many school leavers and graduates not fit to enter the work force) but are unsure of what or how to change. This book explores some of the options.

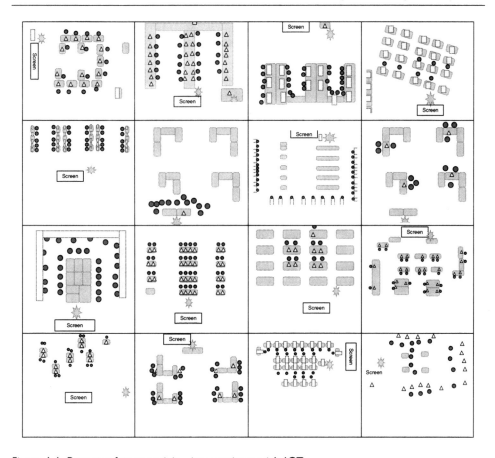

Figure 1.1 Patterns for organising interactions with ICT.

Source: Crook et al., 2010, p. 11. This diagram was provided by Charles Crook for inclusion in this volume, based on that cited.

Note: Circles depict students. Grey blocks are working surfaces. Triangles denote mobile devices and smaller blocks are fixed machines. The teacher (depicted by a star) and screen (labelled) are also shown in most instances. These arrangements were classified in the study as Front-facing, Distributed, Paired working, Small groups, Free-ranging and Waterhole. Front-facing is a common and familiar arrangement and one that is sometimes dictated by the fixed nature of the technology. Other configurations show possibilities for collaborative work or for using a single computer as a site for whole group discussion (the Waterhole). In most project schools each student potentially had access to their own computer and, often, this was a laptop. This allowed the configuration of spaces to be variable and flexible. The free-ranging organisation was an extreme version of the flexibility that small computing devices now allow. It also is a reminder that 'technology' does not simply mean PCs or netbooks. Some class activities depend on access to a variety of technology tools perhaps only briefly.

Summary

This chapter reviews access to digital technology by children and young learners at home and in school and marks the step change that has taken place at the start of the second decade of the twenty-first century. The aspects of digital technology that are particularly powerful when it comes to supporting learning – feedback, editability and communication – are considered. The question is then addressed of what best to do with technology once we reach the point where every learner has meaningful access to a connected digital device at home and in school, a context that could already be realised if schools were more open to the use of personal devices in school.

References

BESA (2013) BESA research reports: *ICT in UK State Schools*. www.besa.org.uk/library/besa-research-reports-ict-uk-state-schools-2013.

Black, P.J. and Wiliam, D. (1998) Assessment and classroom learning. *Assessment in Education*, 5(1), pp. 7–74.

Crook, C. (1994) *Computers and the Collaborative Experience of Learning*. London: Routledge.

Crook, C., Harrison, C., Farrington-Flint, L., Tomás, C. and Underwood, J. (2010) *The Impact of Technology: Value-added Classroom Practice*. Final report. Coventry: Becta.

Dillenbourg, P. and Fischer, F. (2007) Basics of computer-supported collaborative learning. *Zeitschrift für Berufs- und Wirtschaftspädagogik*, 21, pp. 111–30.

Fullan, M. and Donnelly, K. (2013) *Alive in the Swamp: Assessing Digital Innovations in Education*. London: Nesta.

Gee, J.P. (2003) *What Video Games Have to Teach Us about Learning and Literacy*. New York: Palgrave Macmillan.

Horvath, M.A.H., Alys, L., Massey, K., Pina, A., Scally, M. et al. (2013) *Basically . . . Porn Is Everywhere: A Rapid Evidence Assessment on the Effects that Access and Exposure to Pornography Has on Children and Young People*. London: Office of the Children's Commissioner.

McFarlane, A.E. (1996) The effectiveness of ILS, in Underwood, J.D.M. and Brown, J. (eds) *Integrated Learning Systems: Potential into Practice*. Oxford: Heinemann (pp. 15–29).

McFarlane, A.E. (2003) Learners, learning and new technology. *Educational Media International*, 40(3/4), pp. 219–27.

McFarlane, A.E. (2010) Digital creativity – editing versus cheating and how you learn the difference, in Drotner, K. and Schrøder, K. (eds) *Digital Content Creation?* New York: Peter Lang (pp. 149–66).

McFarlane, A.E. and Roche, E. (2003) Kids and the net: Constructing a view of the world. *Education, Communications and Information*, 3(1), pp. 151–7.

Office for National Statistics (2012) *Family Spending, 2012 Edition*. www.ons.gov.uk/ons/rel/family-spending/family-spending/family-spending-2012-edition/index.html.

Prensky, M. (2001) *Digital Game-based Learning*. New York: McGraw-Hill.

Prensky, M. (2012) *From Digital Natives to Digital Wisdom: Hopeful Essays for 21st Century Education*. Thousand Oaks, CA: Corwin.

Rideout, V. (ed.) (2013) *Zero to Eight: Children's Media Use in America 2013*. San Francisco: Common Sense Media.

Sanger, J. (ed.) (1997) *Young Children, Videos and Computer Games: Issues for Teachers and Parents*. London: Falmer Press.

Singapore ICT Masterplan 3 (2011) *Educational Technology Division, Ministry of Education, Singapore*. http://ictconnection.moe.edu.sg/masterplan-3/understanding-the-goals/ict-infrastructure.

Stager, G. (2013) *Stager-to-Go*. http://stager.tv/blog/.

Underwood, J.D.M. and Brown, J. (eds) (1996) *Integrated Learning Systems: Potential into Practice*. Oxford: Heinemann.

US Department of Education, Office of Educational Technology (2010) *Transforming American Education: Learning Powered by Technology*. Washington, DC.

Watson, D.M. (ed.) (1993) *The ImpacT Report: An Evaluation of the Impact of Information Technology on Children's Achievements in Primary and Secondary Schools*. London: DfE and King's College.

Zurita, G. and Nussbaum, M. (2007) A conceptual framework based on activity theory for mobile CSCL. *British Journal of Educational Technology*, 38(2), pp. 211–35.

Chapter 2

Devices and desires

The world is mobile

Smartphones and tablets really are everywhere. Data from 65 countries showed a surge in ownership of these very personal devices in 2013, with smartphone penetration up from 44 per cent to 74 per cent and tablets from 19 per cent to 33 per cent in just one year. The IPG Mediabrands Agency has been investing in an annual global survey for five years and has now collected data from over a billion people across the world with coverage notably missing only from Central Asia and most of Africa. The reason behind this is very telling. The Agency advises on marketing and the surveys seek to understand not just what people do online but also why they do it, in order to better tailor services and products to user needs and thus grow the related markets (Parker, 2013).

This growth in ownership of mobile devices is not restricted to adults. The Wave 7 survey (Parker, 2013) recruited 16–65-year-olds, but surveys by the communications industry regulator Ofcom (2012) in the UK and the Pew Internet and American Life Survey (Madden et al., 2013) in the US suggest the trend is mirrored in those under 16. In 2012 ownership of smartphones among UK 12–15-year-olds jumped to 62 per cent from 41 per cent the previous year and there was a significant though smaller rise in the under-12s. These mobile devices have also become an integral part of life with half the 12–15-year-old users saying this would be their most missed technology, followed by the internet, which they now use more than television. Tablet use is also on the rise with 1 in 7 of 5–15-year-olds using one in 2012 compared to only 1 in 20 in 2011. Together smartphones and tablets are becoming the device children are most likely to use to go online at home. In the US, 50 per cent of children under eight have experience of tablets and both phones and tablets are being widely used in schools:

> 73% of [teachers] surveyed said that they and/or their students use their mobile phones in the classroom or to complete assignments and 45% report they or their students use e-readers and 43% use tablet computers in the classroom or to complete assignments.
>
> (Rideout, 2013, p. 2)

The question then arises of the impact of this increase in ownership and use of connected, mobile devices on support for learning, at home and in school. When 1:1 (one device for each child) device ownership is so widespread, what effect does this have on teacher and student use?

Longer-term studies of the impact of 1:1 ownership of mobile devices are few, not surprisingly given the speed with which the hardware and supporting infrastructure have become affordable and available. However, a number of projects implementing this model of distribution can be found around the world, the best known being the One Laptop Per Child (OLPC) project, born in the US but mainly implemented in developing countries. The OECD has also taken an interest and attempted comparative reviews of work across member countries where personal devices have been supplied to learners and teachers. School ownership of mobile devices more generally has not kept pace with the innovation projects, and there is unease around the Bring Your Own Device (BYOD) model due not least to the variation in the technology and the problems of providing meaningful access to wireless networking. Contexts outside school where up to a thousand users might want to access media rich content simultaneously, invariably resort to fixed networking, putting the 1:1 school's need for an application of wireless at the edge of what the technology was designed to support. This is rarely a good place to be if the need for reliability and low cost are paramount, as they always are in schools. The lack of reliable, affordable wireless networking in schools has been identified by the British Education Suppliers Association (BESA) as a key barrier to uptake of ubiquitous computing in schools (BESA, 2013).

However, there have been evaluations of trials of mobile technologies and there are ongoing projects supplying class sets of tablets. These evaluations provide valuable lessons on what is likely to work, how these devices can be used to enhance learning and the pitfalls to be avoided in a successful implementation. One thing is abundantly clear – it is not enough to simply have the devices, just because they are there does not ensure they will be used to good effect.

Getting the most from mobile devices in schools

Research into the implications of 1:1 device distributions in schools reveals some common themes that seem to persist across contexts. Here I draw primarily on a three-year study that colleagues and I carried out for the UK government agency for education and communications technology (McFarlane et al., 2010). The study followed a cohort of children in years 5 and 6 (age 10 and 11) in two regions of the UK as they were given wireless-capable, handheld devices for their exclusive use at home and in school, and then followed them as they transitioned into their first year of secondary school. The devices used were at the leading edge of functionality and could do most of the things a tablet could do in 2013, including capture and play video, albeit on a smaller screen more akin to the mini-tablet. The key findings match those emerging in earlier reviews and later projects such as the

Tablets for Schools programme (Naismith et al., 2004; Faux et al., 2006; Wishart et al., 2007; Tablets for Schools, 2013).

Our research found that as with all innovations with technology, it takes time to establish effective use of mobile devices in a classroom and even more time for this to spread within a school. The technology must be reliable, robust and flexible. All users, teachers and learners, must be competent with the device. Teacher continuing professional development (CPD) must include basic operation of the device on its own and with a network and offer clear examples of effective use within the classroom. One or two examples of powerful applications are enough to seed uptake. The use of video of effective practice from classrooms, especially of teachers in the same school or area, proved especially powerful for demonstrating these examples. Not all teachers will be natural innovators but, with support, those who are can be champions for meaningful device use.

The research captured a range of device use that was effective, innovative and supportive of teachers and learners. After two years, clusters of active use clearly showed the potential for these devices. However, these uses do not inevitably become universal or habitual. It is difficult for device use to become embedded if devices are unreliable and there are problems with the wireless connectivity. Also, where teachers cannot rely on all students in a lesson having a working device, they make using the device optional, so that learners without a device (it may be broken, left at home or with a flat battery) can still take part. The result is that the unique strengths of the device may not be fully exploited. Another barrier is the mismatch between device use and assessment (McFarlane, 2003). Formative assessment may still be paper based – teachers mark work in exercise books but not on the device – and high-stakes assessments rely on handwriting skills, which leads some teachers and some learners to concentrate on paper-based work, especially as external assessment points approach. Nonetheless, learners clearly associate the use of mobile devices with learning, in school and out of school. Moreover they see the devices as supportive of effective learning, even where their own levels of use are low, and this persists over time so is not simply an effect of novelty.

Why 1:1 mobile devices?

Whatever model of teaching and learning was in use, it was clear that their response to the device itself shaped the attitudes of teachers and learners. The small size and the potential for personalisation that ownership made possible meant that many learners developed a strong and intimate relationship with this learning tool.

In addition to its mobility, the idea of 'everything in one place' (work done, resources collected, tools such as cameras, software and applications easily available), was frequently cited as a positive by learners and teachers. Teachers felt this enabled them to be more flexible in their planning and fluid in their teaching, able to seize learning opportunities more easily. The device enabled them, for example in a science investigation, to take photographs or video, log data on a spreadsheet, have access to the internet and make notes. In performing arts, physical education and modern foreign language lessons the video and audio recorders were used to capture performance for evaluation and improvement. Although all these activities are possible with a digital camera and a laptop, the fact that they could be achieved with a device the learners had with them meant that teachers were more likely to use them as, because everyone had one, they could use a more learner-centred approach. Teachers were glad to be relieved from the burden of having to book equipment or computer access, the constraints of timetabled lessons in the computer room and the added complexity of juggling with limited sets of equipment.

Each learner having their own device also made possible whole-class interactions between the devices and the interactive whiteboard, for example through the use of response software where each learner can input to a multiple-choice question displayed on the whiteboard. This increased learner participation and also helped teachers to monitor development of understanding or spot misconceptions, thus leveraging the use of equipment already installed in the classroom to greater effect.

Features that support learning

Across our studies certain features associated with the 1:1 ownership of the device emerged as valued by students and teachers to support learning. Device use was seen to:

- facilitate individual, co-operative and interactive work in class;
- enable the sharing of knowledge, ideas and responses;
- increase participation in whole-class settings;
- enable learners to revisit for repetition, consolidation and reflection out of the classroom on things introduced in class – this helps to increase understanding;
- provide opportunities for autonomy and independence;
- permit storage of work and resources all in one place and to hand;
- enable the transfer of work between digital devices;
- alleviate pressure on the computer rooms and make learning more flexible.

At all levels pupils reported they were more likely to show school work to family members when it was via the device. Having work on the device also meant they were more likely to revisit it themselves. When the device also supports connection to the school learning platform (see Chapter 4) the possibility of having all work in one place and being able to reflect on it and show others will be even greater.

Understanding competence

There is a temptation to see children and young people as natural users of technology and assume competence where it may not exist. Research also suggests that learners are not always very good at assessing their own level of expertise either so simply asking them if they can use a device can be misleading – getting some response from a device is not mastery. In reality most learners need support in becoming effective users of the device and particularly in using the device to support their learning. Apparent expertise often collapses on investigation and it is unwise to assume that interaction with the device will automatically be effective. Patterns of use of devices vary, with some learners enthusiastic and frequent users, in and out of school, for learning and other personal purposes. Other students in the same class may make very little use. Some learners become active and effective users of devices to support their learning with little apparent support, but on investigation it emerges that most have had help, which may come from teachers or support staff in school, family or friends. A lack of understanding of how to use the device is a key factor in non-use. Learners for whom a supportive context for developing expertise is not available, at home or among friendship groups, and who are not pro-active in seeking help are much less likely to be effective users.

The need for training

Professional development of teachers in the effective use of connected devices to support learning is fundamental to a successful implementation of 1:1 mobile computing. The projects we documented used a variety of models from issuing devices to teachers over a summer break and assuming they would return fully competent in their use (they didn't), to providing a buddying system in school with regular group workshops with teachers from other project schools, which worked well. Adequate and appropriate training that supports the development of a collaborative, self-supporting community of practice is likely to increase the impact of any 1:1 project. A whole-school approach, with support provided both for the project activity and for those implementing it, contributes to device use being embedded across the curriculum. This requires time and resources and a recognition that teachers' needs vary and they move at different speeds. A focus on 'training' in operating the device can leave too little time for understanding learning processes facilitated by 1:1 provision and engaging with challenging questions raised by device use. The least confident teachers need evidence, models and examples of effective use. The more engaged risk-takers want time for reflection, sharing and discussion.

For students (as for teachers), having a device was not sufficient to ensure productive use for learning. The assumption that 9–12-year-olds were 'digital natives' and would therefore take easily to device use did not prove to be well-grounded. Overall, the extent of device use in each context was the result of a complex of inter-relating factors: skill and confidence in device use; requirement by teachers for use in lessons and for work out of school; availability of support from home and peers; patterns of use, interest in and attitudes to digital technologies at home and among peers. Where requirements for school-related use, audits of skills and specific strategies to support uses for learning (including drawing on the experience of previous users) were not present or were under-developed, overall usage levels remained low. Lack of skill and confidence among teachers exacerbated this.

Parents and peers

The extent to which any individual learner mastered their device depended strongly on the skills and attitudes of those they mixed with at home and school. Most learners sought help with their device from friends and family and the balance of this varied from school to school (see Table 2.1).

Evidence from parents confirmed the wide variations in use reported by students and the suggested connections with home and peers that affected this. We then looked at the relationship between level of use and source of support in some detail in the year 6 students (age 11) who had had devices for two years. There is a marked correlation between the level of help from family and friends and the overall level of use (see Table 2.2).

In particular, low users do not get support from their family, and are less likely to get it from their friends. We did not collect data which would allow us to report on level of use related to overall learning ability, but we did meet students who

Table 2.1 Sources of help in learning to use the device

	My family help me with the device (%)	My friends help me with the device (%)
Primary school A	47	76
Primary school B	17	77
Primary school C	50	69
Secondary school D	34	77
Secondary school E	85	87

Table 2.2 Sources of help in relation to levels of use as reported by year 6 pupils

	Strongly agree/agree		Strongly disagree/disagree	
Usage	Family help (%)	Friends help (%)	Family help (%)	Friends help (%)
High	62	83	26	10
Medium	45	69	25	16
Low	0	60	55	25

struggled to learn to use their device. One particular interviewee told us that using her device was just another thing she was not very good at. Clearly if mastery of the device is a challenge, family cannot offer support and friends also struggle, it is easy to see that these factors can combine to create a major barrier to using the device. Similarly, if there are family members who are users and can support the learner, friends who are keen to share ideas and experience, and learning comes easily the situation is set for a very positive outcome. With such wide variation in competence and access to support possible in one classroom, it is important that schools monitor use and competence levels in a way that is sensitive to the complexities and have strategies for supporting low or non-users through a buddying system and/or offering training sessions to parents.

A technique we used to investigate individual levels of use and competence was for a researcher to sit with a learner for a short time and invite them to show their device and talk about something of their choosing they had done with it. The ensuing conversation very quickly revealed the level of competence with the device and the level of work being produced with it. Such short exchanges could easily be introduced into pastoral or tutor time so that each learner's ability to use their device effectively to support their learning could be monitored and a learning plan developed to suit their needs.

Parents, who are often asked to support device acquisition in 1:1 projects and are likely to be the source of the majority of devices in a BYOD model, are generally in favour of 1:1 projects, although there may well be some who are not and a school needs to be alert and sensitive to this. We did see a small number of cases where parents were clear they did not want their child to have a device, and this was not a matter of cost but rather connected to beliefs about technology and, in some cases, learning. Clearly such parents need to know the school's position on technology before committing their child to attend since accommodating individuals who do not work with technology within a school that has become technology-enabled will be very difficult for all concerned.

Parents appreciate communication from school about device use and opportunities to ask questions and hear from teachers. There remain some concerns in society at large around the amount of time children and young people spend using screen-based technology, and dialogue with parents can help to establish appropriate models and levels of use and better equip parents to support device-based learning at home. Both at home and in school it is also important to ensure adequate time away from screens interacting with other people and the real world.

Impacts on learning

With extreme caution, our research suggests a possible association between frequent use of a mobile device, where it occurs, and positive attainment. Teachers reported that device use, for some students, led to increased engagement and focus, which was beneficial to learning. Overall the data suggest an association between frequent use of the device and meeting or exceeding the school's expected levels of attainment at the end of the year. In addition, where teachers made frequent and thoughtful use of the device in lessons, there appears to have been a positive effect on student attainment as monitored by teachers. These teachers reported that, for some students, being given more choice in using the device as a tool to accomplish goals and present their work led to increased engagement and focus, which was beneficial to learning. There are contra-indicators and exceptions and further research is needed to better understand these. Achievements in the only standardised tests used in the time our research took place, at age 11, could not be mapped to use at an individual level. Some high-level users achieved beyond their predicted grades, others did not. Similarly some low-level users exceeded their predicted grades and others did not. Again, further research is needed to better understand this variability and what exactly the role and nature of device use might be in this.

Personal devices in primary school

Having an authentic purpose for use of the devices is central to the success of implementing personal technologies to enhance teaching and learning in primary schools. Teachers should be clear about the exact learning goals they are hoping to achieve when using these technologies – these may be as much about the culture of learning as about specific content or skills. Although some successes have resulted from models of use where not every learner has a device, or where the devices are not 'owned' by learners, teachers find it harder to manage meaningful use of devices in a whole-class context when not everyone has one.

There is no doubt that teachers play a key role in pupil uptake and use of devices. Only small numbers of young learners spontaneously begin to use devices to support their learning – in or out of school. Where teachers are making regular use of devices in class a majority of learners will use the device under direction and autonomously both in and out of class. Where pupils still fail to use their device even though their teachers are encouraging them in class, a lack of competence in using the device is a major barrier. These students do not work out how to operate the device, neither do they seek out help, for example, from teachers or support staff or pick up these skills from friendship groups or at home. There is a need to identify these learners and provide support to make sure they know how to operate the device competently. This is perhaps more easily achieved in a primary context where a small number of teachers spends large parts of the school day with the same children.

In contrast, some learners are often sophisticated users, making informed choices about when and when not to use their device. Their conclusions may, however, be very different. For example some learners prefer to use the device to produce text, they use spell check and predictive text, incorporate images in their work, value the appearance of this work and find it easier than handwriting. Others prefer paper, which they find easier to use and feel they need to practise handwriting. This may also be associated with poor keyboard skills and a view that the screen of the device is too small. These different approaches can be found in learners who are in the same school and even the same class.

Most learners value the ability to access the internet for research using the device. The only pupils who do not seem to value this have high levels of access to very good alternative technologies in the home. Projects that have tested the use of mobile technology to build links between home and school and to increase family involvement have had most success where the level of home access to technology is low. In cases where home access is already high, a very specific role for the personal devices may be more effective, for example, to carry information between home and school.

Teacher attitudes to device use continue to vary even within one school in some cases. It is clear that the majority of teachers needs to be shown effective examples of exactly how the devices can be integrated into lessons. The possibilities for device use in developing an iterative (and more independent) model of learning (see Chapter 5) were not established in any of the projects we saw, even after two years of use, not least because this was not an explicit aim for the school. The teachers who innovate with devices are exceptional. Supporting these teachers to share their insights provides benefits to all those involved in a project. Moreover, providing opportunities for teachers to work with those who can offer technical insight and support has resulted in major breakthroughs and developments of new applications for device use.

The transition to secondary school

Some primary schools involved in 1:1 projects expressed concerns that the children who had become active users in the final two years of primary school would find the move to secondary school more challenging, especially where they were no longer part of a 1:1 pilot. Research by the author and colleagues at the University of Bristol focused on a cohort of over 120 children with previous experience of 1:1 ownership of a mobile device for at least one and usually two years in primary school as they made the transition to secondary school. We compared the practices of the children with previous experience of device ownership to those of their classmates who had not been part of any 1:1 project in primary school.

In year 7, aged 12, these children experienced three different contexts for access to ICT in secondary school. One cohort joined a school where they were issued with a new model of mobile device on a 24/7 ownership model, a second cohort entered a school where there was no access to mobile devices and a third went to a school with some access to mobile technologies in school but as a pooled resource. Almost all of the children from the primary 1:1 projects retained their mobile device and we documented varying patterns of persistent autonomous use in each of the three secondary scenarios.

In spite of differences in the demographic of the schools and the socio-economic backgrounds of the students, the technological context at home was very similar. Internet access was almost universal and a wide range of digital technologies was owned or available. However, there was a marked variation in the frequency and range of *use* of digital technologies reported by individuals. Interestingly, previous experience of mobile devices was not a significant factor in this. High, medium or low frequency users of digital technologies included those with and without primary-school experience of mobile devices. Again this underlines that access and use are not the same thing.

Use of digital technologies in school was dependent on school policy, and on access to technology and teachers' practices, which varied within and between schools. Previous out-of-school users used mobile devices more for personal purposes; most students used their devices for school learning only when required by a teacher. In general, use of all digital technologies was only partly associated with competence and inclination. Whether a student (irrespective of gender or level of attainment) was a frequent, moderate, infrequent or rare user was affected most by the attitudes and expertise available in the immediate and extended home context, and among peers. It seemed more important to operate within established norms.

There were indications among some previous and new users of mobile devices that 1:1 ownership can support an orientation to using and managing digital technologies for independent learning. However the research suggests that without direction, support and the provision of models by teachers, the majority of students do not spontaneously develop these skills and practices or carry with them from primary-school habits they developed there.

In summary there is no guarantee that students who have established a pattern of device use to support their learning in primary school will carry this with them to secondary school. A culture of use in school needs to be the norm and encouraged by teachers before learners will make autonomous use in class even when they have the skills and experience to do so. Out-of-school use of the device to support learning may persist among the really keen but again unless this is encouraged and supported it is unlikely to persist. Previous users were strongly present among students from the three schools who reported activities that suggested an orientation to using and managing digital technologies for learning: writing/taking notes, revision, games for learning, organising files, finding information. This might indicate a carryover of practices developed in the primary phase but was also true for some students with no such experience. Among students who were new to mobile devices in year 7, those who became the frequent users were very likely to exhibit these same behaviours. As with much else, beneficial experience in primary schools needs to be recognised and encouraged if it is to persist and contribute to learning in the secondary context.

Factors affecting uptake in the secondary setting

Aspirations for the secondary projects we worked with were that 1:1 mobile device use would emulate and develop the primary experience of some students in enhancing motivation and encouraging independence in learning. Also it was hoped that having devices would encourage a pedagogic shift to more active and collaborative learning and exploit the anytime/anywhere potential for learning. Most students expected that device use would have a positive effect on lessons and learning.

Due to the more subject-based management of teaching in secondary schools, 1:1 projects tended to be run in a small number of departments or with a particular year group. This presented difficulties since neither learners nor teachers had sufficient, consistent opportunities to use the devices. Unlike in the primary context where the children used their devices all the time with a small number of teachers, the secondary students might have one or two lessons a day, if that, where teachers even referred to the technology. Unsurprisingly, the impact was very patchy as a result.

Outcomes were varied. There were notable successes and strong endorsement of the value of 1:1 device ownership. However a number of factors, some technical and external to the project, affected successful exploitation of the potential of the device in teaching and learning. These barriers had a huge impact on the extent of take-up, especially in lessons. They included:

- Screening by the internet service provider whereby only websites previously registered could be accessed. This proved frustrating for teachers, students and parents and, although this strategy may have achieved its e-safety objectives, it compromised the utility of the internet connectivity.
- Some specialist subject websites in regular use did not yet have versions for access by mobile devices and so could not be used any more widely than before.
- The differences between mobile versions and PC versions of standard applications were seen as presenting users with additional and demotivating challenges.
- The failure of the device to be linked to the school's learning platform meant that there was no easy way to move digital work around. This affected the amount produced and its incorporation in assessment for learning.
- The perceived pressure of curriculum and assessment targets created tensions and dilemmas around device use for some teachers and students. There was minimal use of the device beyond the classroom and sustained and collaborative projects were relatively rare.

The first year did not deliver wholesale pedagogic shift but there was experimentation and change that was welcomed by many learners. The teachers who most wholeheartedly took up the challenge used their professional expertise to explore how the potential of the device might be best incorporated in the learning cycle. In general they were convinced of the value of the device in teaching and learning and for some the experience quite radically affected their practice. Teachers less confident about the device or less convinced about its value were more inclined to make device use fit established practices and schemes of work.

Frequency of use of digital technologies overall was dependent on school policy, access to technology, and teachers' practices. In this secondary context, activity was dominated by internet searching and making presentations. Students were more likely to use technology to support learning out of school where they had experienced teachers modelling effective use in the classroom. Overall, students reported more use of digital technologies out of school than in school, and more use for personal purposes than for school work, supporting the idea that frequent technology users are required to 'power down' when they enter school. The range of activity reported out of school by most students included playing games, internet searching, listening to music and instant messaging. More creative uses of digital technologies were reported by some of the most frequent users, which fits with the common patterns described in Chapter 6.

In general students were dependent on teacher direction for school-related use out of school. Notable exceptions to this were associated with use of mobile devices to 'go over' or clarify work done in class. Students who found this helpful included some previous users who had transferred to schools where mobile devices were not supported as a tool for learning. They had retained their device and re-visited work done in the primary phase. Where mobile devices were supported in year 7, experienced users continued this practice and new users developed it. In general teachers were not aware of and did not plan for or encourage such activity, which makes this element very unusual in this regard.

What does this say about the future for the personal device in school?

With the price of tablets, laptop computers or equivalents falling, and learning platforms supporting access beyond school becoming widespread, there is inevitably a question as to whether a device that can be carried in the pocket and held in the hand will be significant. It is important to remember some of the key functions of the smaller devices that make their use in schools practical:

- the battery lasts all day, which cannot be over-emphasised as a key factor since managing flat devices is a major barrier to use in schools;
- they are always there and instantly on – again a major factor as time to boot up can be another issue in class;
- carrying all your 'stuff' with you is important to users; and
- many learners already have them.

Many tablet devices share this set of features and the fundamentals emerging from studies of the use of these newer devices reveal a very similar set of conclusions to our mobile study, and a degree of neutrality as to the actual device so long as it is personal, mobile and connected. It is the case that the ability to access the internet individually in lessons (without having to go to a computer suite or book a set of laptops) is utilised widely in secondary where the school culture permits; the activity could often have been done on any connected device, laptop, tablet or smartphone. Equally homework set could be done on a desktop or laptop (and frequently is).

When learning platforms provide every student with a space for storing work and materials, the use of a personal device to transfer work between home and school may become redundant. Families may also be able to get easy access to students' work by logging onto the learning platform; one of the current advantages of personal devices that is valued by some students and their parents is looking at work together. However, the data stored on the device include work in progress and a mix of personal and public content and so may go beyond what would be on a shared platform. The device belongs to the learner and is with them 24/7, opening up the possibility of opportunistic learning, such as a bit of maths practice while waiting for a parent.

The mobility of the device is important within school and between home and school but with the current curriculum and assessment regimes commonly in operation, we have as yet seen relatively little planned use for learning outside the classroom. The mobility of the device has been exploited on primary-school camp and in secondary work experience modules but these are exceptions rather than established practice. The opening-up of the curriculum to learning based on greater integration between subjects, the development of vocational courses and work-based elements, the focus on personalisation: all of these recent moves could be well-served by mobile 1:1 device ownership. In addition, the roll out of virtual learning environments (VLEs)/learning platforms in schools may mean a school-wide endorsement of digital work, which could encourage innovations in effective assessment for learning, and make tracking of out-of-school learning more realistic.

Maximising the chances of success

Our research suggests the following advice for schools planning a one device per child project:

- To maximise the benefits of personal ownership, pedagogical approaches and teaching styles must accommodate a more autonomous learner role.
- The curriculum itself needs to accommodate this new attitude to learner responsibility for the approach to learning.
- The most successful projects combine the use of the device to access curriculum content and to produce student work in a variety of media, and lessons are planned to take advantage of both use and production of content.

- The time taken to manage the devices, in projects with personal ownership, takes up very little class time once the devices are established, leaving more time for the wider educational objectives of the lesson.
- Good integration with existing technologies in the school, e.g. interactive whiteboards, data projectors, software and digital content, aids the smooth adoption of the devices into routine teaching and learning.
- Having an authentic purpose for use of the devices is central to the success of implementing personal technologies to enhance teaching and learning.

Although some successes have resulted from models of use where not every learner has a device, or where the devices are not 'owned' by learners, teachers find it harder to manage and it is important to have small numbers of spares to make sure everyone has a working device. Make sure the devices used are:

- robust with a battery that lasts all day;
- compatible with the school learning platform;
- running all software commonly used in the school for teaching and learning;
- affordable with spares so everyone has one working all the time;
- personal to the user.

Invest in technical support and ensure adequate wireless connectivity and an appropriate internet service.

Ensure training of staff, students and family members where needed so that everyone is familiar with the functions of the device needed for learning. Training for teachers must also extend to use for effective teaching and learning. Recognise that teachers and students each have different needs and that any training needs to account for this. Encourage collaboration between learners to get the most from their devices.

Choose a model of implementation that fits the culture of teaching and learning the school aspires to and teachers can exemplify.

Allow time for the cultural shift, be inclusive in the planning but make sure that leadership articulates a clear vision and that this is not optional.

Summary

Personal ownership of powerful mobile devices has now reached the point where the majority of adults in OECD countries own at least one and they are the preferred device of under-16s. These devices could be used to support learning in schools and this chapter distils the learning from two longitudinal, large-scale studies of learners in primary and early secondary education who enjoyed 1:1 ownership of a device for at least two years, including as they transitioned between schools in some cases.

The importance of support in learning to operate a device and to use it to support learning is shown through the different outcomes for those students who mastered this and those who did not. The role of family and friendship groups is highlighted. The perceived benefits, barriers to success and variables affecting uptake and use are discussed, and the factors that maximised the chances of a successful implementation are identified.

References

BESA (2013) *Tablets and Apps in Schools*. London: BESA. www.besa.co.uk.

Faux, F., McFarlane, A.E., Roche, N. and Facer, K. (2006) *Handhelds – Learning with Handheld Technologies*. Bristol: Futurelab. www.futurelab.org.uk.

McFarlane, A.E. (ed.) (2003) Assessment for the digital age. *Assessment in Education*, 10(3).

McFarlane, A.E., Triggs, P. and Yee, W.C. (2010) *Researching Mobile Learning*. Coventry: Becta.

Madden, M., Lenhart, A., Duggan, M., Cortesi, S. and Gasser, U. (2013) *Teens and Technology*. Washington, DC: Pew Internet and American Life Survey.

Naismith, L., Lonsdale, P., Vavoula, G. and Sharples, M. (2004) *Literature Review in Mobile Technologies and Learning*. London: Futurelab.

Ofcom (2012) *Children and Parents: Media Use and Attitudes Report*. http://stakeholders. ofcom.org.uk/binaries/research/media-literacy/oct2012/main.pdf.

Parker, G. (2013) *Wave 7 – Cracking the Social Code: The Story of Why*. IMG Mediabrands Agency. https://dl.dropboxusercontent.com/u/3503218/Flipping-Books/Wave7/index.html.

Rideout, V. (ed.) (2013) *Zero to Eight: Children's Media Use in America 2013*. San Francisco: Common Sense Media.

Tablets for Schools (2013) *Stage 3 Research Report*. www.tabletsforschools.org.uk/stage-3-research-report-available-for-download/.

Wishart, J., Ramsden, A. and McFarlane, A. (2007) PDAs and handhelds: ICT at your side and not in your face technology. *Pedagogy and Education*, 16(1), pp. 95–110.

Chapter 3

Public spaces

Everybody's online

It is fair to say that educational technology pundits did not, in the main, predict and were somewhat slow to spot the explosion in what have become known as social media. These tools allow an individual to share anything from a stream of short messages to a multimedia diary of every personal detail with anyone from close friends and family to the entire online world. While these products were being devised and growing huge followings, the eyes of educational technology were firmly fixed on their much tamer cousins, the VLEs, of which more in Chapter 4.

At the time of writing something like one in seven people on the planet has a registered account with the leading social media provider, Facebook. No doubt that product will lose, and some argue is already losing, its market position at some point and users will flow into other online spaces, but it seems the ability for individuals to communicate in the broadcast model pioneered by Facebook is likely to persist for some time to come. Indeed Facebook, Twitter and their ilk have changed the way social interactions take place at a fairly fundamental level. When 12–15-year-olds claim that their smartphone is their most significant technology and preferred way to go online (Ofcom, 2012), it is surely the use of online communication with their social network that is paramount here.

As with any activity undertaken by the young in large numbers and with zeal, society at large has some concerns about the resulting effects and the mainstream media carry many scare stories. Concerns around the use of social media coalesce around four main issues: once posted, content in a social media account can never be entirely erased; access to individuals 24/7 with the option of anonymity has fuelled a culture of cyberbullying; unfiltered online access is exposing young people to a range of inappropriate content, particularly pornography; and young people may be contacted by, or make contact online with, those who wish them harm. Given all of the above, what are the implications for education, both in preparing young people to be safe, active and effective users of social media and in using these tools as a way to support their learning?

Assessing the risks – audience and etiquette

What could possibly possess anyone to post photographs of themself online, clearly wildly drunk or in some other state that they would not want their granny to see? It is easy to dismiss this as the act of an unthinking youth who cannot imagine ever having a job interview, or a career, or children of their own, or that their granny even knows how to go online, and clearly there is an element of youthful exuberance behind such actions. The difficulty is that once posted to a social media site, the poster no longer has control of that image. Not only can it be sent on to many more people than originally intended, and seen by their networks, it cannot be erased. It is there for ever as a permanent record. The follies of youth do not disappear into the past, each post becomes a potential virtual albatross around the neck of the poster or anyone else involved or implicated.

At the time of writing there are various movements in the US and Europe seeking legislation that will change this situation. One proposed option is that anyone under 18 will have the right to delete permanently content they have posted. A landmark ruling in Europe in 2014 established the idea of 'right to be forgotten' which may ultimately change this, although once content is distributed it is hard to see how this could be enforced. An alternative to legislation is to reduce the risk by making sure that young people have a better understanding of what they are doing in the first place and some appreciation of the consequences. Understanding the security settings on a social media account is one place to start. This can determine who can actually see an individual's content and chooses to be alerted whenever something new is added. Or at least up to a point, since if content is re-posted, additional networks will be able to see it immediately. The result is that it is never possible to be entirely sure who can see material that appears on the social media space of a given individual.

The following scenario gives a flavour of the unintended consequences that can arise as a result. You send an amusing photograph shot on your phone, of the two of you, to a close friend – perhaps not a very flattering image, or one you might later want to erase. Your friend finds this very funny, and posts it on their social media page. At this point it is now entirely out of your control who sees this image, who copies it and where it ends up. Suddenly the whole class, year group or school has a picture of you in the pink pyjamas your mum gave you for Christmas, seemingly having forgotten you are 16 not 6. Not quite so funny now. And there was not even any malicious intention, just a moment of thoughtlessness, and in this instance the consequence is embarrassing rather than more serious. Had the original image been more intimate and the friend's intentions less benign, the end result could be more severe. Thinking through the possible consequences of where images can end up might help young people to resist the pressure to share intimate images via the phenomenon of 'sexting', which is alarmingly prevalent among teens (Ofcom, 2012).

Social media has opened up a whole new set of ways we can and do impinge on one another and as yet there are no hard and fast rules of engagement. Indeed we seem, in the English-speaking world at least, to have abandoned most of the rules we used to use to manage social engagement in the face-to-face world – formal etiquette is a thing of the past. This is perhaps not an entirely bad thing as many of the rules were restrictive and seemed designed to keep people in their place – but the result is that we are often rather at a loss and can be inconsiderate of one another, pushing past one another, not holding doors open for people, interrupting or using a mobile when engaging with another person. School remains one of the few places where socialising behaviours in the real world are still taught and expected and norms can be established. Surely this is also where we should be expecting some common rules of engagement online to be at least discussed and debated from an early age. When agreeing a set of rules by which we treat each other with consideration and respect, which is a common activity in many schools, we should also be adding some rules that apply in online settings. Indeed, advice from the Department for Education (2013) in England recommends involving children and young people in the development of their school's e-safety policy and highlights four basic principles relating to keeping personal information private; thinking about the long-term view of content posted; never posting inappropriate, offensive or illegal content; and abiding by website rules such as age restrictions. Never post online something you would not want read out or held up in class is a useful maxim.

Cyberbullying

Cyberbullying takes the name-calling and mean behaviour of the school playground to a new level as those with a grudge are able to send messages via a range of routes, private and public, over the internet and by phone. The public posting of such material adds to the discomfort and humiliation, and the reach extends into the home and school holidays as youngsters are increasingly online permanently through mobile devices. The Cyberbullying Research Center in the US has been collecting data on trends in antisocial online behaviour since 2002. It points out that reported levels of experience of cyberbullying among teens in published sources varies from below 3 per cent to over 70 per cent but its data suggest there is wide variation with an average of 27.4 per cent, close to the average across other published reports. It also collects data on the bullies and found that an average of 17 per cent of students have engaged in bullying behaviour (Patchin, 2013).

In 2013 the charity Ditch the Label, in partnership with Habbo Hotel, launched an annual survey of cyberbullying (Ditch the Label, 2013). Ditch the Label is a charity concerned with combating prejudice and bullying, based in the UK with an international reach. Habbo Hotel, as the largest online global community for teens, hosted the survey and over 10,000 users took part from the UK, US and Australia for the main part. Even allowing for possible bias – those affected by the issues may be more likely to respond and the survey was accessed through the help section of Habbo Hotel that Ditch the Label supports – the results were stark, with seven in every ten respondents experiencing cyberbullying and one in five subject to this on a daily basis. In the UK alone if that ratio is indeed indicative of the wider population, 1.26 million young people are subject to hurtful communications every day. This is no longer restricted to the playground taunts of traditional bullying but pervades every moment as messages pop up, unbidden, on the mobile phone. Home and school holidays no longer offer any respite, which intensifies the impact of unacceptable behaviours. This surely contributes to the report by 70 per cent of the sample that their self-esteem and social lives are being affected catastrophically as a result. The results were remarkably stable by age and gender, although those reporting as transgender suffered twice the incidence of the rest of the sample.

Levels of bullying varied across the different social media being used but all of the services the survey sample reported using had some incidence. There is a clear association with the ability to post anonymously, with sites that do not support this option being less likely to inadvertently host cyberbullying. It is not surprising then that pressure groups are calling for an end to the phenomenon of anonymous posting. Quite how that would work is yet to be thrashed out, as a move to a situation where children and young people could be traced through their online activity by anyone with a desire to do so is unlikely to improve the safety of minors online. It is possible to imagine, however, a situation where a registered, legitimate source – a school head teacher, for example – could request the identity of an individual on production of proof of the posting of inappropriate content. Or even simpler, it should always be possible to flag to the service provider when damaging content has been posted, so it can be removed and the poster cautioned or, for grave or repeated offences, banned. So even where controls are in place to reduce the risk of cyberbullying, it is still vital that this is a topic that is openly discussed and debated in schools and where parents are equipped to support children who are victims, or perpetrators, of digital attacks. Not least, the line between legal and illegal behaviours in online (and offline) communications should be made clear. Given the high profile of a number of cases that have had tragic consequences for the victim, awareness of the phenomenon is now high and there is a range of online resources to help parents, teachers and those involved to identify and support those affected. The first highly publicised criminal trial in the UK, as a result of online threats, led to the imprisonment of the two perpetrators and raised awareness of the gravity of such behaviours.

Pornography

In 2013 researchers at Middlesex University produced the report of a rapid assessment exercise on the effects that access and exposure to pornography has on children and young people (Horvath et al., 2013), carried out to inform the Inquiry into Child Sexual Exploitation in Gangs and Groups by the office of the Children's Commissioner in the UK. The report covers a literature review and the outcomes of two workshops with experts and young people to test the conclusions of the draft review. In this case children and young people include anyone up to 18, up to 24 for looked-after children and up to 25 for those with a disability. The distinction between access and exposure is significant, with access being deliberate and exposure being non-deliberate or coerced viewing of pornographic material. In this context the following definition of pornography was used: 'Sexually explicit media that are primarily intended to sexually arouse the audience' (Malamuth, 2001, p. 11, 817).

The conclusions are stark and worrying. It seems that pornography is becoming more 'hard core' with images depicting violence and degrading behaviours common. Content suggests a norm where males are aggressive and dominant and females are submissive and the subject of abuse and humiliation. Not surprisingly there is a difference in the way different gender groups respond with girls being far more concerned and uncomfortable about porn and boys being more engaged and seeing porn as having a benefit, 'but there is some emerging evidence indicating that young people are dissatisfied with the sex education they are receiving and that they are increasingly drawing on pornography, expecting it to educate and give information regarding sexual practices and norms' (Horvath et al., 2013, p. 8). This is perhaps the most worrying finding as it suggests that schools and parents are leaving children and young people insufficiently informed about their own sexual identity and what they can and should expect from sex and relationships. Young people are turning to porn as an alternative, with exposure reported from as young as 10 in some cases. As a result they are adopting as normal many behaviours that are outside those likely to be practised in a healthy, consensual relationship and are more likely to engage in high-risk behaviours such as casual, unprotected sex and 'sexting', the sending of intimate, personal images via mobile phone.

It is telling that of the seven recommendations that emerge from the Horvath report, three relate to the legality of pornographic content, but three of them are directed to the Department for Education and one to the government more generally, which has implications for education:

1   The *Department for Education* should ensure that all schools understand the importance of, and deliver, effective relationship and sex education, which must include safe use of the internet. A strong and unambiguous message to this effect should be sent to all education providers including: all state-funded schools including academies; maintained schools; independent schools; faith schools; and further education colleges.

2   The *Department for Education* should ensure curriculum content on relationships and sex education covers access and exposure to pornography, and sexual practices that are relevant to young people's lives and experiences, as a means of building young people's resilience. This is sensitive, specialist work

that must be undertaken by suitably qualified professionals, for example, specialist teachers, youth workers or sexual health practitioners.

3 The *Department for Education* should rename 'sex and relationships education' (SRE) to 'relationships and sex education' (RSE) to place emphasis on the importance of developing healthy, positive, respectful relationships.

4 The *government*, in partnership with internet service providers, should embark on a national awareness-raising campaign, underpinned by further research, to better inform parents, professionals and the public at large about the content of pornography and young people's access of, and exposure to, such content. This should include a message to parents about their responsibilities affording both children and young people greater protection and generating a wider debate about the nature of pornography in the twenty-first century and its potential impact.

(Horvath et al., 2013, p. 11)

This last point raises an interesting question in relation to the safeguards available in the home and school to protect young people from exposure to undesirable content. Ofcom (2012) reports that over 70 per cent of UK parents have rules in place to govern children's use of the TV, internet, mobile phone and gaming. However, barely half were using the parental controls provided on computers, and multichannel TV services. Web filters on phones or gaming consoles were even less common. Most parents do talk to children about safety online and only 15 per cent of parents made no attempt to intervene in media access, but 48 per cent show some uncertainty as to whether they know enough to advise their children appropriately. But none of this may matter in the end as the Ofcom data showed no difference in likely or actual risky online behaviour among children regardless of parental rules or technical mediation through filters, passwords, and so on. It seems that despite our best endeavours children and young people need help to avoid risk online and to cope with disturbing content should they access or be subjected to it, as simply trying to protect them from access or exposure is not working.

Learning to be safe online

Research studies suggest that most young users of social media have little or no interest in communicating online with people they do not know. While somewhat reassuring, this still leaves a percentage who are vulnerable to strangers and much adverse exposure comes via people who are not strangers at all. Additionally, cyberfraud is a major and growing crime, difficult to police and often international in nature. It is never too early to learn to be cautious online.

The picture from research is one of children and young people spending more and more time online, increasingly via personal, mobile devices, which suggests more private access than say via a family computer in a shared space or at school.

Further, despite parents' attempts to talk to them about the risks or use technological mediation to minimise exposure to undesirable content, under-18s are just as likely to see content that they may not want to, or which would be deemed unsuitable for them where no such restrictions are in place. It is unacceptable to assume that children and young people are so 'tech-savvy' that teachers should get out of their way as Prensky proposes (Prensky, 2001, 2012) Not only are assumptions about technical prowess often misguided (see Chapters 2 and 6) but also clearly there is a need for social and moral education around safe and appropriate use of online environments. There is also a need for suitably trained professionals in the education system, which will necessitate the training of teachers.

In 2008 an OECD council of ministers considered the issues surrounding online access to content, which resulted in recommendations adopted by the OECD council and published in 2012. These recommendations seek to tread the line between supporting under-18s to benefit, along with over-18s, from the free flow of information afforded by the openness of the internet and protecting minors from engaging in behaviours that put them at risk, those who might seek to harm them, aggressive direct marketing and exposure to unsuitable content. The OECD calls for national policies on internet use and coalitions of service and content providers with policy makers, with research and monitoring of effectiveness of the measures taken over time. It specifically suggests:

1   Integrating Internet literacy and skills in school curricula with a focus on risks and appropriate online behaviour;
2   Training educators and encouraging other stakeholders to educate and raise awareness of children and parents;
3   Regularly measuring the evolution of their Internet literacy.

(OECD, 2012, p. 10)

The United Kingdom Council for Child Internet Safety (UKCCIS) offers a forum for a range of organisations interested in children's welfare and industry partners as well as CEOP (The Child Exploitation and Online Protection centre). These all offer free resources for parents and teachers via their websites, they are up to date and will certainly help any interested reader to keep up with the latest trends and issues as well as understand how the most popular social media operate and how to work any security options available. UKCCIS was founded following a major review of children's use of the internet and particularly video games by Tanya Byron (Bryon, 2008), which raised awareness of some of the issues around unsafe and unsupervised use. The subject of digital games and learning is covered further in Chapters 5 and 7.

Fitting into a busy curriculum

Schools are called on to include more time for coverage of RSE, online citizenship, and technical competence with a fast-moving and complex array of tools and services. All of this requires space in the curriculum as well as time for educators to keep their own skills and knowledge up to date, and in the case of dealing with the inter-personal elements to engage with specialist training. This is against a background where schools in many countries in the developed world are struggling to produce a population of school leavers with adequate basic numeracy and literacy to join the workforce (OECD, 2013). Nonetheless, given the consequences for such high numbers of young people and the risk level of damaging experiences online, from friends and strangers, there is a powerful argument for making space in a crowded curriculum to learn the rules of safe and responsible online citizenship, and how to deal with the effects of the seemingly inevitable encounters with those who do not practise it. There is a widespread call from parents, policy makers and learners themselves to make time for online citizenship as well as including internet use in relationship education, and to up-skill teachers in both. This is part of the wider issue of digital literacy, which is a cross-curricular matter. Just as there is a risk of a computing or information and communications technology (ICT) curriculum ghettoising issues of effective use of online content (Chapter 5), in the same way there is a need for the awareness of what it means to be a safe and responsible user of social media to be embedded in the broader culture of school and home use.

Developing a culture of e-safety

As use of connected digital services and online media by children and young people becomes commonplace, intelligent use of them becomes a core element of learning to integrate into wider society. Knowing how to behave towards others and keep yourself safe while being socially and ultimately economically active are key life skills. As part of their duty of care, schools have a responsibility to prepare learners to be safe and effective users of the internet and wider digital services to support their learning and to operate in their lives outside school and, ultimately, the world of work.

A national policy on computer use in schools has been a part of the education landscape in many OECD countries for some decades. There has been a tendency to identify work using computers within a dedicated curriculum block, in a subject such as computing, information technology (IT) or ICT. In some cases defined curricula have been produced, indeed in the UK a new subject of Computing came into force in 2014/15. The result of this policy focus, coupled with the relative scarcity of computers usually grouped in computer suites, has meant that computer use in schools has been restricted to dedicated lessons – largely about the technology itself and how to operate it. More widespread use in a range of subject contexts is growing as device access increases, and the trends described here in Chapters 1 and 2 are likely to speed up the potential for this.

The dual drivers of increased use of digital technologies in schools to support learning and almost universal social and leisure use result in an urgent need for schools to have a culture of informed and responsible use embedded in the wider ethos of the school and explicitly stated within the behaviour policy. Fortunately this need has been recognised and there are many sources of help and support for schools available. I have identified two providers below and explained why I think they are worth identifying, pointing out the kinds of information and service that parents and educators should be looking for when evaluating a potential source of information and support.

360 degree safe

In the UK the South West Grid for Learning (SWGfL) has published a framework against which schools can audit their current position in relation to policy and practice in e-safety called 360 degree safe. Having established where they are, the framework also acts as a road map for improvement. Strands deal with Policy and Leadership, Infrastructure, Education and Standards and Inspection. The last, Inspection, may be particular to England, but the rest have universal relevance. Indeed, SWGfL consulted with experts in the US as part of the process of defining the self-review framework. Its website also offers a range of resources to support schools in designing and implementing an e-safety policy.

A strength of the SWGfL approach is that it helps to make clear the who, what and how of e-safety. Everyone has a role; this is not the sole job of a subject co-ordinator or the technical support staff. Job descriptions for all staff should make their contribution to e-safety explicit. Learners and parents are required to sign up to usage agreements. Policies are living documents, made widely available and reviewed regularly. All of this takes time, and there may be a temptation to put this to one side, or leave it all in the hands of the computing teacher, but the stakes are too high for that. No one individual, or department, can possibly ensure a consistent cross-organisational approach to safe and effective use of digital technology. Schools are used to developing and implementing acceptable codes of conduct on a range of issues from behaviour to uniform, and together these shape the culture of the school. The leadership comes from the top, the vision is shared and everyone signs up to it. Transgressions are noted and acted on. E-safety has to become an embedded part of that culture, as the 360 degree safe framework makes very evident.

Common Sense Media

In the US the non-profit organisation Common Sense Media offers information and advice to parents and educators about safe and effective use of media by children and young people. It offers a view of digital media as the 'third parent' based on the view that children spend more time with screen-based media than either at school or engaged with parents and that this affects their development, socially and intellectually. It takes a very pragmatic view that we 'cannot cover children's eyes, but we can help them to see'. The message is all about taking responsibility. Policy makers, media and service providers are not let off the hook either.

Modelling online citizenship

When in school it is reasonable to expect school staff to model the behaviours and habits expected within the school community. Schools and parents expect certain standards of dress, language, attitudes and behaviours towards learners and other staff and so on. The exact nature of these standards may vary from school to school and across countries, but they will exist and teachers and learners who are not prepared to accept and abide by them will at best have a rather unhappy time and at worst find themselves excluded.

Social media bring life beyond school into the classroom in an unprecedented way. While there have always been expectations of those working with the young in terms of their overall conduct, the minutiae of their daily lives were most likely a private matter. Bumping into pupils when you popped out for a pint of milk in your slippers was about as much as you had to contend with as a teacher. Now it is all too easy for parents and pupils to view and publicise the digital footprint of a member of the school staff. Moreover, that footprint, perhaps better described as a tattoo, is not just current material but potentially anything that has been posted by or about them. Indeed it is entirely possible that before making an appointment, a school may and arguably should carry out a review of the candidate's online history. This is, of course, one of the potential pitfalls schools will be educating their own learners to avoid but for would-be teachers it may be too late.

So, perhaps more than most, teachers need to be very thoughtful about their own use of digital media, what they post and where this might end up. They also need support not only to manage incidents of cyberbullying of those they teach, but also in how to manage the consequences of being harassed themselves. This is likely to cover a wide range of possible interactions with pupils, from emails asking for help with homework arriving at all times of the day or night, to parents making requests. It is important to establish rules of engagement. When and how often staff are available to accept contact from pupils and parents, which email addresses are shared, what response times can be expected, all of these need to be made explicit and form part of a contract between teachers, learners and parents and carers. Used well, digital media can support a coalition between young people and those who support them in and out of school. Used badly, 24/7 communication can become a nightmare of unmet expectations and the constant pressure of a bulging inbox.

Summary

The advent of social media has seen a revolution in the way young people communicate with one another, and the results are not always pretty. Some research suggests one in five young people are subjected to negative messages on a daily basis, nearly as many also admit to cyberbullying. This chapter looks at the problems of bullying and inappropriate content online and the role schools can take in educating students to be good cybercitizens. This is not simply something for the computing class but an important element of wider school culture. The chapter concludes with two examples of services set up to support schools and families in their quest for e-safety, and a discussion of the importance of modelling the practices of responsible online behaviours across the curriculum.

References

Byron, T. (2008) *Safer Children in a Digital World*. London: DCSF.

Department for Education (July 2013) Principles of e-safety. www.education.gov. uk/schools/pupilsupport/pastoralcare/b00198456/principles-of-e-safety.

Ditch the Label (2013) *The Annual Cyberbullying Survey*. www.DitchtheLabel.org.

Horvath, M.A.H., Alys, L., Massey, K., Pina, A., Scally, M. et al. (2013) *Basically . . . Porn Is Everywhere: A Rapid Evidence Assessment on the Effects that Access and Exposure to Pornography has on Children and Young People*. London: Office of the Children's Commissioner.

Malamuth, N. (2001) Pornography, in Smelser, N.J. and Baltes, P.B. (eds) *International Encyclopedia of Social and Behavioral Sciences*. Amsterdam: Elsevier, vol. 17, pp. 11,816–21.

OECD (2012) *The Protection of Children Online*. OECD. www.oecd.org/sti/ieconomy/childrenonline_with_cover.pdf.

OECD (2013) *OECD Skills Outlook 2013: First Results from the Survey of Adult Skills*. OECD Publishing. http://dx.doi.org/10.1787/9789264204256-en.

Ofcom (2012) *Children and Parents: Media Use and Attitudes Report*. http://stakeholders. ofcom.org.uk/binaries/research/media-literacy/oct2012/main.pdf.

Patchin, J.W. (2013) *Summary of Our Research (2004–2013)*. Cyberbullying Research Centre US. http://cyberbullying.us/summary-of-our-research/.

Prensky, M. (2001) *Digital Game-based Learning*. New York: McGraw-Hill.

Prensky, M. (2012) *From Digital Natives to Digital Wisdom: Hopeful Essays for 21st Century Education*. Thousand Oaks, CA: Corwin.

Chapter 4

Collaborative places

The rise of the online learning experience

Perhaps the defining digital technology of the early twenty-first century has been the collaborative online space. These tools have given a potential voice to every online citizen to broadcast or respond to every other person online. The most familiar are the social media sites, where billions of users post personal information or form interest groups to share content on a chosen topic, which can be literally anything at all from rocks to rock cakes to rock stars and all points in between. The ability to find others with a shared interest, anywhere in the world, is perhaps one of the real strengths of social media. Very quickly, corporate interests adopted the tools and techniques of social media, adding the facility to comment or post content to their websites, and web 2.0 was firmly embedded in our lives. Education was also quick to adopt similar tools with the VLE taking root in the university sector and then evolving into versions aimed at the school level. VLEs are now to be found in a number of guises in schools at all levels, even at pre-school.

One difference between the educational tools and those more widely available is that users have to be 'enrolled' in the space and their identity is verified by the host organisation. Only those entitled to join a school or course are given access through a unique username and password. This provides some security and protection for users from unwanted contact and the less-pleasant effects of anonymity that can occur in open systems (see Chapter 3). In these environments, even where a user can post anonymously, everyone is known to the administration and inappropriate use can be tracked and managed. The better-designed systems offer users space to store work and resources over time, to collaborate through discussion that supports more than the 140-character posts of the microblog and to comment directly within another person's content, and includes tools for multiple authors to work on shared documents. The systems are designed to support a social model of learning, where work is stored, shared, commented on, discussed and revisited. Ideally the system also integrates with the management information system (MIS) so that learner records can be kept centrally and matched to their performance data.

The early models of VLE use in universities were slow to develop and very often the system became little more than a shared, virtual filing cabinet. Tutors would create a space for a course, enrol the students in it and post all the resources for the course electronically including content such as the presentations used in the lectures. Coursework might subsequently be submitted through the VLE but social constructivist models of learning, where work was shared in draft and commented on by the tutor and other course members, or where active online discussions were part of the experience, were less common. The exception was in distance learning models where providers such as the Open University in the UK were early adopters and pioneered models of effective learner engagement (Salmon, 2000). Contemporary VLEs are a key element of the apparent explosion of the MOOC (massive open online course), a new development that has been sweeping the global higher education space in the first decades of the twenty-first century. But the attempt to use VLEs to revolutionise the campus experience, as student numbers rose and staff numbers remained static, was yet another example of the failure of a model where the technology is simply presented to users with assumptions made about the technical competence and, perhaps more important here, the models of teaching and learning in play, which proved to be barriers to full exploitation of the theoretical potential of the tools. It remains to be seen the extent to which the MOOC model actually replaces on-site provision in higher education or whether it represents a different form of provision that will take its place alongside the traditional format.

The outcomes of adoption of VLE use in the university sector offer useful lessons on avoiding the pitfalls in the adoption of collaborative learning environments in schools. First and foremost, the tools and the culture of teaching and learning in the school must be mutually supportive. The vision for the school must be clearly articulated, led by the head teacher and shared by the staff. It must be explained to pupils and parents, and valued by them. The model of technology use by teachers and learners must then fit this vision.

What can a VLE do for a school?

A VLE, or learning platform, offers a secure online space with tools to support access to resources and content and to facilitate communication between those enrolled. VLEs may come as an off-the-shelf package or consist of a suite of products that offer appropriate interoperability, that is, they that work together. An example of the latter might include a mathematics tutorial suite that shares performance data with an MIS used to track learner progress. I will not attempt a review of current products, first because this would quickly date and second because it would fill a book on its own. What I will attempt here, however, is an analysis of the functions these systems offer and how they can be used to support effective teaching and learning.

A good VLE will offer a navigable storage system through which teachers can signpost and students can access a range of content and tools. The content may be produced in the school, by teachers or learners, purchased from a commercial source, pointed to via a weblink, and so forth. These will be arranged using a shared structure, which everyone is inducted into using. A common structure might group resources by subject (or subjects), year group, class or set, date used, and so on, and ideally can be searched through any such labels.

Access to resources can usually be controlled by the teacher/administrator so that each learner or group of learners sees the material relevant to them rather than the whole bewildering array. This is where integration with the pupil data management system is vital. Class or set lists should be generated once and then used to set up learning groups within the VLE. Similarly, any performance data generated should be stored securely with the unique pupil record. This integration of pupil data and curriculum content caused real concerns around security and integrity of data in the early days of computers in schools, with some schools running separate networks for administration and curriculum use. Contemporary systems should have good enough internal security to protect users and their data. Re-keying fundamental data is to be avoided wherever possible as it is fraught with difficulty, time-consuming and prone to error.

How well such a resource will work in a given school will depend very much on how well teachers and learners are trained to use the system and the development of common protocols for use. Clearly if resources are to be shared, users must use the same terms to label the same or similar things. Conventions for version control are vital. If a user tweaks a resource then overwrites the original this can cause frustration and time wasting. It is also likely to lead to individuals keeping their own copy of key resources, which takes more storage space and again increases the chances of errors creeping in. Where pupils' work is also being stored, the file names must be consistent and differentiate each individual's work and the version of it. If a whole class save their work as 'MathsClassbMonday.doc', or an individual saves everything as 'Sam's stuff', the results will be tears all round. These simple, basic conventions need to be thought through, taught and policed. Also the whole staff needs to take ownership of the system if it is to work well. Such simple protocols can make the difference between the effective, school-wide use of a learning platform and a poor implementation of the same product set, which adds little value.

The VLE should offer effective spaces to share work in progress, ask questions, discuss issues and generally collaborate. Learners and teachers should be able to set up shared spaces for classes or smaller groups to use. Communication tools should integrate with those already commonly in use, for example, by sending alerts when new messages are posted, as without this there is an inclination to bypass the VLE and use established tools. This dilutes the interactions with the rest of the experience and makes it harder, if not impossible, for tutors to intervene. Collaborative learning is a much-researched area, and CSCL research has its own, very active, global community. One thing that is clearly evidenced through this research base is that collaboration aids learning, but it is unlikely to be spontaneous. Learners must learn to collaborate and be set tasks that require them to do so. None of this is likely to happen across a school unless there is a shared vision for effective teaching and learning that values and embeds collaboration. Without that, no matter how powerful the available digital tools that support such methods, they are unlikely to impact beyond a few more maverick teachers' classes.

A vision of collaborative learning for schools

For some years there has been a somewhat sterile debate in education that presents skills and knowledge as alternative starting points for curriculum design. This is unhelpful to both policy makers and practitioners. At the very least there can be no such thing as a 'content-free' curriculum since any learning must involve a context and substance. To develop skills a learner must practise them using content. Further, rote knowledge with little or no understanding of its relevance or purpose is clearly of very little utility. This oppositional debate, prosecuted by political and academic factions across the world as they debate policy that defines the school curriculum, has not helped schools to make intelligent use of technology. Neither has it helped to progress a coherent vision of technology-supported learning fit for the world school students inhabit and will emerge into as young adults. Things become a little clearer if knowledge is viewed as something humans *create*, and that this process of knowledge creation is something all learners can engage in and with. Moreover, an important component element of knowledge is content – to know is to know something! These seemingly simple ideas can be used as the basis of a powerful model of learning and teaching.

The key to this idea may be the use of the term 'create'; indeed this may be the bridge between the curricula that have dominated developed world school systems in the late twentieth century and those that are struggling to emerge in the twenty-first century. The test-driven systems prevalent particularly in the US and UK are beginning to break down. Levels of achievement have stagnated, following early apparent rises, and standards of pupil behaviour deteriorate year on year according to annual reports from the UK Chief Inspector of Schools published by Ofsted over the last 20 years and the international PISA (Programme for International Student Assessment) comparisons (OECD, 2013). This overall decline clearly has causes beyond the school system but a curriculum that offers little authenticity to learners does not help. There is evidence that learners are increasingly bored by school and engagement with school drops sharply as students progress through the grades (Fullan, 2013). As long ago as 2002, in response to the lack of creativity in the UK curriculum, the (now defunct) Qualifications and Curriculum Agency (QCA) in England offered a view of the kinds of pupil thinking and behaviour that would be involved in creative learning:

- Questioning and challenging
- Making connections and seeing relationships
- Envisaging what might be
- Playing with ideas
- Representing ideas
- Evaluating the effects of ideas
  (Taken from QCA Creativity Pack information sheet 3, September 2002)

It is very significant that these behaviours are clearly not unique to the traditionally creative elements of the curriculum, those that deal with the arts and crafts, for example. Indeed this approach to learning could be easily applied irrespective of the subject area under study and clearly echoes Scardamalia's notion of working with and improving ideas as being at the heart of knowledge building (Scardamalia, 2000). Moreover, it goes beyond the concepts of procedural knowledge, and what is usually called constructivism in the classroom with its emphasis on problem solving and project work. Here knowledge is something to be worked on and with, not an entity to be passively consumed or even individually constructed. Perhaps this is the most important aspect of the nature of knowledge we need to grasp in order to inform a curriculum that is both relevant and engaging for learners growing up in the digital age.

Importantly, this way of working with ideas is inherently social, involving as it does discussion and argument, justification and exploration. This makes school an ideal site for such learning, where learners meet and engage in fast-paced discussions and exchanges of ideas that are much harder to achieve online and do not arise spontaneously when the only contact is digital (see Chapter 5). Bereiter (2002) suggests that this opportunity for social learning, along with childcare, may be the most powerful reason to retain schools as sites of learning in an information-rich age. Arguably, the Kahn Academy in the US, which has adopted a 'flipped classroom' model, is an implementation of this approach. Here students study content at home and come to school familiar with the content knowledge they need and questions they have and are thus prepared to take an active part in debate and other social tools of learning as they engage with fellow learners in a facilitated peer group to work out what they have learned actually signifies.

The challenge to schools is to build a model and culture of learning that works locally and that links meaningful theories of knowledge to models of education. Moreover, these models of education cannot preclude a role for defined content, or the absence of a range of existing forms of effective teaching such as direct instruction, but rather weave these into a fabric that builds on what is good in the current system and takes it forward to embrace personal and collective knowledge building. For without coherent, scalable models of what is it to teach and learn using meaningful knowledge practices, no matter how convincing the theoretical arguments, schools are unlikely to enjoy success in the terms that broader society is prepared to recognise and policy demands. That success demands acceptable high-stakes test scores and, at the same time, preparation to be economically and socially successful in a digital world.

Digital technologies in a knowledge-building curriculum model

One of the most powerful, and often overlooked, affordances of digital technology is the ability to record, copy and edit data sets, from a word-processed document to a digital video, with an ease that is unmatched in the equivalent non-digital media (see Chapter 8 for an elaboration). The ability to work with ideas, evolving and honing one's expression or interpretation of them, until a personal understanding and accurate articulation of that understanding have been achieved is at the heart of the constructivist view of learning. It is also the mechanism underpinning the creative process and has proved to be a vital element in the knowledge-building programmes of Scardamalia and Bereiter (2003). Furthermore, working iteratively in this way, individually or collaboratively, with review and comment from peers or experts, is at the heart of the process of formative assessment – which has proven power in the improvement of learning (Assessment Reform Group, 1999; McFarlane, 2001, 2003). An environment that supports learners and teachers to store, review, comment on, revise and develop content in a range of formats, to manage change over time, to comment and discuss, must surely be a vital tool in a school that seeks to develop a culture of active and productive learning, enjoyed by reflective and thoughtful teachers and learners. So why are they not universal in schools, what is holding up progress and how might these barriers be overcome?

Cheating or poor citation?

There is concern that learners are using online sources to simply cut and paste content or even to download complete assignments to pass off as their own (McFarlane, 2010). A survey carried out by the Association of Teachers and Lecturers (ATL) and published in 2008 showed that over 50 per cent of their members believe that plagiarism is a major problem in student work. The greatest source of problem content is, of course, the internet. Just as digital texts offer the author an easy way of editing her own content, they also offer ways to copy and paste others' content into a personal text with even greater ease. In a small study carried out in the UK through the BEEP (BioEthics Education Project) (Wishart et al., 2007 and see www.beep.ac.uk) teachers of post-16 students reported that these students lack skills in information filtering and quality assessment. In particular, students

- don't question the authority of information sources;
- don't like to think;
- cut and paste without engaging.

If this is as widespread in schools as the ATL study suggests, it raises some serious questions as to how, if at all, these students are being taught to use information to develop personal knowledge. Certainly it is difficult to reconcile this situation with one where the students are indeed being taught to use information sources appropriately.

It is in this context of discussion and debate about the exact nature of the ideas being presented and explained where the real difference between editing and cheating becomes a lived experience. There is little room for unthinking incorporation of other people's content in the cut-and-paste culture described in the ATL study when you know that, first, this is likely to be evident to and exposed by one's learning community and, second, you are likely to be challenged to explain or amplify the text you have posted.

Alone together: the would-be collaborative learner in formal education

Throughout the sixty plus countries that make up the OECD, testing and international comparisons are important influences on national education policy. Testing cultures tend to focus on the level of the individual – not the group. This has profound implications for the model of the learner, who is treated as a lone consumer of content to be reproduced on demand in the context of the test. This view in turn impacts on learners' beliefs about themselves as learners, the nature of meaningful learning and the role an individual needs to play in order to be successful within formal education. The game is to pass tests; what counts as useful knowledge is only that which contributes to test passing, and the trick is to learn only what you need to pass the tests. This has a significant and negative effect on learners' attitudes to education (Harlen and Deakin-Crick, 2002). The notion of education as personal enrichment is entirely lacking; learning serves an external purpose and the outcome is a certificate that entitles the holder to move to the next level. Learners who have experienced this model of education at school are likely to carry it with them into further and higher education, and even at postgraduate level will often focus only on that which is assessed. If the only purpose of formal learning is to pass externally set tests, the learner has no responsibility for or ownership of their learning for its own sake – the experience lacks personal authenticity.

This can be contrasted with a view of the curriculum that does not focus solely on familiarity with pre-defined content, but on the ability to find, analyse and appraise relevant content, and construct coherent, justified views that could be construed as personal knowledge. This approach can be used with a wide range of content and in a wide range of contexts, from nursery to postgraduate levels. This is often mistakenly taken to mean that this approach is at odds with a defined curriculum where factual content is specified and familiarity with it is tested. It is easy to see that in a constructivist model access to content remains essential, but learning does not equate solely to familiarity with a pre-defined body of content. It is the job of the learner to aggregate, analyse and assimilate relevant content. The tools and skills to locate, compare, critique and construct are what is needed here and the internal coherence and validity of the produced text and related conceptual artefacts are paramount. One contemporary justification of this productive model of learning is that this approach to personal knowledge building is highly relevant to those who live in the age of the internet. As availability of content grows ever faster, it is not enough to have a fixed body of personal knowledge. It is vital to be able to update, modify and extend one's picture of the world. The necessary knowledge practices embedded in a productive model of learning are those that will best prepare learners to take an active part in modern economic and social activity.

Moreover, these knowledge-building skills are best honed in a social context, working with others to explore, test and refine ideas. In this model, knowledge is socially constructed and in this kind of learning environment, as Goodyear (2001) has pointed out, the roles of the teacher and student change. The teacher is no longer the main source of unchallenged declarative knowledge, rather she becomes a consultant, guide and resource provider. Teacher expertise is in asking good questions and giving meaningful feedback and facilitating learning interaction rather than providing all of the answers. The teacher is predominantly a designer of student learning experiences rather than a provider of content. In this changed environment, the learner must take some responsibility for their own, and others', learning. They must see themselves not as passive receptacles for hand-me-down knowledge but as constructors of their own knowledge, who refine their own questions and search for their own answers through interactions with others.

Valuing fellow learners

In a learning culture that focuses on the performance of the individual, and identifies the teacher as the more capable other, as in Vygotsky's (1978) socio-cultural theory of learning, there can be resistance to working with peers. The teacher is seen as the authority whose feedback and comments have value. Interaction with a fellow learner may not be seen as useful. And yet it is not always necessary to know more than a fellow learner to be able to help them refine their thinking, and your own. Asking good questions is at the heart of effective teaching and it is entirely possible to ask good questions without a full understanding of the subject under study. Seeking clarity, asking for justification and requiring supporting explanations for statements, talking about varying views, explaining: these are among the interactions between learners that can help all involved to improve understanding and expression.

There has been much popular comment on the difficulty for teachers of this change in culture, and the need for training to develop new pedagogical models. As a result the need for professional development is a recurring theme in national policy dialogues. Some commentators seem to assume that the transition is easy, or at least easier, for the students, who are, after all, the children of the information age, used to high levels of access to information and communications technologies. However, this change of roles is not easy for the student either, as research has shown, and seems to require far more than facility with the technology itself (e.g. Walker, 2004; Cox et al., 2004; Soller, 2004; Thornham and McFarlane, 2011).

As Woolgar's (2002) first rule of virtuality states: 'The uptake and use of new technologies depend crucially on local social contexts.' And as Crook and Light's (2002) study from the same programme, on virtual society and the cultural practice of study, illustrates, student study habits have changed as they use computers and other digital devices simultaneously to access a range of resources and applications, not all of which are related directly to study. Yet they see themselves primarily as learning alone when they are not in class. So to assume that the use of internet technologies to chat with friends, listen to music, search for resources and check the precise assignment brief on the course VLE simultaneously while working on the assignment on a word processor, may indeed represent a change in knowledge-building practice, but it has not changed the learners' perception of themselves as lone learners or of learning as an essentially solitary practice. Moreover, when students do choose to collaborate using electronic communications they will tend to eschew the tools offered to them, such as discussion boards in online learning environments, and stick to good old text, social media and internet chat. This model of themselves as working ultimately alone to build personal knowledge is, of course, the model that informs the assessment process. Ultimately high-stakes awards are made to individuals not groups. Indeed at the school level there is a thin line between working collaboratively and cheating. So it is not surprising that students struggle to find new ways of working collaboratively simply because they are using a computer-mediated communication environment. Even making posting to the discussion board an assessment requirement is not enough (e.g. Cox et al., 2004). There is a clear tension between the ways of working and the manifestations of knowledge that are credited and those that are required in a collaborative learning environment online or offline. Although students may be invited to discuss, debate, offer views and support arguments, they remain reluctant to do so online (e.g. Walker, 2004) perhaps in part because they see themselves ultimately as judged individually.

Models of meaningful collaborative learning will only operate where the culture of the classroom adopts a respectful, interactive model of discourse between learners, the tasks set are appropriate and the model of management of time and space permits and encourages productive interaction. Learners have to learn to learn effectively together and be helped to see the value in this and how it contributes to their own individual performance. Only then will they be capable of drawing on the rich resource that is their fellow learners either face to face or online.

Summary

Tools to create online collaborative learning spaces, VLEs, first developed for use in colleges and universities, are now widespread in schools. This chapter looks at the potential of such powerful tools to support a model of learning built on personal knowledge building, and argues for that model as an appropriate preparation for life in a digital, information-rich and ever-changing world. The importance of collaboration in learning and the value of peer-to-peer interactions are discussed. Finally, a few pragmatic but often overlooked details for the effective management of work in a VLE are offered.

References

Assessment Reform Group (1999) *Assessment for Learning: Beyond the Black Box.* Cambridge: University of Cambridge, School of Education. http://cdn.aaia.org.uk/content/uploads/2010/06/Assessment-for-Learning-Beyond-the-Black-Box.pdf.

Bereiter, C. (2002) *Education and Mind in the Knowledge Age.* Mahwah, NJ: Lawrence Erlbaum.

Cox, G., Carr, T. and Hall, M. (2004) Evaluating the use of synchronous communication in two blended courses. *Journal of Computer Assisted Learning*, 20(3), pp. 183–93.

Crook, C.K. and Light, P. (2002) Virtualisation and the cultural practice of study, in Woolgar, S. (ed.) *Virtual Society? Technology, Cyberbole, Reality.* Oxford: Oxford University Press (pp. 153–75).

Fullan, M. (2013) *Stratosphere: Integrating Technology, and Change Knowledge.* Toronto: Pearson.

Goodyear, P. (2001) *Effective Networked Learning in Higher Education: Notes and Guidelines.* http://csalt.lancs.ac.uk/jisc/guidelines_final.doc.

Harlen, W. and Deakin-Crick, R. (2002) *A Systematic Review of the Impact of Summative Assessment and Tests on Students' Motivation for Learning.* London: EPPI Centre.

McFarlane, A. (2001) Perspectives on the relationships between ICT and assessment. *Journal of Computer Assisted Learning*, 17(3), pp. 227–35.

McFarlane, A.E. (ed.) (2003) Assessment for the digital age. *Assessment in Education*, 10(3), pp. 261–6.

McFarlane, A.E. (2010) Digital creativity: Editing versus cheating and how you learn the difference, in Drotner, K. and Schrøder, K. (eds) *Digital Content Creation?* New York: Peter Lang (pp. 149–66).

OECD (2013) *PISA 2012 Results in Focus.* www.oecd.org/pisa/keyfindings/pisa-2012-results-overview.pdf.

QCA (2002) *Creativity: Find It, Promote It.* London: QCA.

Salmon, G. (2000) *E-moderating: The Key to Teaching and Learning Online.* London: Kogan Page.

Scardamalia, M. (2000) Can schools enter a knowledge society? in Selinger, M. and Wynn, J. (eds) *Educational Technology and the Impact on Teaching and Learning.* Abingdon: Research Machines (pp. 5–9).

Scardamalia, M. and Bereiter, C. (2003) Beyond brainstorming: Sustained creative work with ideas. *Education Canada*, 43(4), pp. 4–7.

Soller, A. (2004) Understanding knowledge-sharing breakdowns: A meeting of the quantitative and qualitative minds. *Journal of Computer Assisted Learning*, 20(3), pp. 212–23.

Thornham, H. and McFarlane, A. (2011) Discourses of the digital native: Use, non-use, and perceptions of use in BBC Blast. *Information, Communication and Society*, 14(2), pp. 258–79.

Vygotsky, L. (1978). *Mind in Society: The Development of Higher Psychological Processes*. Cambridge, MA: Harvard University Press.

Walker, S.A. (2004) Socratic strategies and devil's advocacy in synchronous CMC debate. *Journal of Computer Assisted Learning*, 20(3), pp. 172–82.

Wishart, J., la Velle, L., Green, D. and McFarlane, A. (2007) The opportunities afforded by online discussion for teaching bioethics in secondary schools. *School Science Review*, 88(324), pp. 59–65.

Woolgar, S. (ed.) (2002) *Virtual Society? Technology, Cyberbole, Reality*. Oxford: Oxford University Press.

Chapter 5

Solving problems, building knowledge

Growing up in the knowledge society

The first invention that allowed us to encode and transmit information without a physical courier to take it from one place to another was the telegraph, devised at the very end of the nineteenth century. This was the first time that the obstacles of distance and geography were removed from communication, so that messages could be received almost instantaneously across thousands of miles over oceans and mountain ranges. Subsequent developments in information technologies through the twentieth and early twenty-first centuries define what has become known as the information age. During that time the pace of invention has been dizzying as digital technologies become smaller, faster, more powerful and cheaper. Today instantaneous communication worldwide is available through a device you can hold in your hand, without the need for wires or specialist knowledge. That same device can access more information than can be held in any library and even transmit text, sound, still and moving images and is cheap enough for a majority of the developed world to own one.

There are those who argue that the advent of these technologies has changed the nature of knowledge, and of knowing (Lyotard, 1984; Lankshear et al., 2000). Indeed there are some who believe the way the mind works when using such technologies is different and that this has implications for brain development in the young (Greenfield, 2004). Few dispute that knowledge creation fuelled by unprecedented access to information is or is predicted to be the basis of wealth and economic growth for the first half of the twenty-first century. Potentially we are raising a generation who think differently and preparing them to live and work in a world much changed from that of their parents' and grandparents' childhoods. As a result of this there are widespread calls for the education system to change to better prepare learners to take their place in a 'knowledge economy' that supports the 'knowledge society'.

This call for changes in approaches to policy and practice is set against an out-of-school context where most school-age children in the developed world have very high levels of access to a range of digital technologies (see Chapter 2):

- almost all have access to a computer outside school;
- most have internet access and much of this is broadband;
- social software is very popular;
- most enjoy digital games;
- most have their own mobile phone;
- in school most get to use technology for a small fraction of the time (once a week on average in Europe);
- most use digital technologies to support school-related learning out of school.

However, it is dangerous to assume that this physical access equates to deep and meaningful use of these technologies. The rhetoric that proposes that *all* young people are so-called digital natives, enjoying rich and complex creative interactions with and through digital technologies, is mere techno-romanticism (see Chapter 6). While a majority is certainly engaging with digital and social media, they do not automatically acquire the skills and knowledge to benefit fully from the potential for powerful learning that these opportunities afford.

This situation raises some interesting challenges for schools. A small but significant proportion of young people is developing meaningful skills in creating and sharing content and engaging with rich problem solving, for example in games contexts. If, as seems likely, these experiences and the skills and knowledge developed as a result do indeed give an advantage to those who have such access, what are we/should we be doing in school for the ones who are not? Moreover, how do we keep the attention of those who are? What should the tasks that sit at the heart of the learning process in a knowledge society look like and how should learners be supported to enact these tasks successfully?

Beyond the skills vs. knowledge debate

There is a somewhat baffling debate among those interested in education as to whether a school curriculum fit for a digital age should focus on the development of specific content knowledge or on the skills needed to work meaningfully with information, the learning to learn agenda. Given that it is impossible to work with information in a vacuum, you have to have some content to work with, and content knowledge without the understanding to use it effectively is pretty pointless, the skills vs. knowledge dichotomy breaks down on even cursory examination. Moreover, when meeting new information a key difference between the novice and the expert is the existing body of relevant knowledge they have available to contextualise, interrogate and generally make sense of the new content. Skill in learning or information handling is therefore inextricably linked with content knowledge. Any curriculum must address both what is to be learnt and how it is to be taught and learned. The extent to which a statutory curriculum defines a common body of content for all is at least partly an ideological issue and therefore likely to remain something of a political football. Unfortunately the way in which that content is taught is also largely ideological and reliable evidence on effectiveness of different approaches is hard to find and always contested.

At the heart of the curriculum debate there are three issues that I would argue are more important than the skills vs. knowledge question:

1   the way in which learners meet content;
2   the processes through which they assimilate this into personal knowledge; and
3   the evidence they are required to present to be accredited with their resulting learning.

These are the factors that make the difference between an education that prepares young people to be flexible and thoughtful learners, ready to work with new information and in novel contexts, and those who are largely practised only in reproducing what they have already met. In this chapter I want to consider the implications of these differences for pedagogy and the ways using digital tools in the classroom can support a less traditional approach to the process of learning. First I will look at the changes in pedagogy that might better fit a knowledge society, then look at three uses of digital tools that can help teachers to manage that approach in the classroom.

Changing pedagogy

There have been many attempts to capture the essence of the changes in knowledge and knowing that have resulted from the advent of the information age, and the implications of those changes for pedagogy. One model that has informed my thinking and research behind this chapter is that of Voogt and Pelgrum (2005) shown in Table 5.1.

This model captures the key elements of pedagogical shift likely to result in the kind of learning and skill development that would equip individuals and groups to be socially and commercially successful in an information-rich culture as they develop the capability to create personal knowledge. This model also echoes the aspirations of those implementing technology-enhanced learning interventions including objectives such as enhanced learner autonomy and collaborative learning (McFarlane et al., 2007). There is, crucially, a call for a move from reproductive learning, where what is learned is produced to order, to productive learning where learners tackle novel problems and create their own representations of knowledge and understanding, individually and collectively.

While the move from an industrial to an information age is widely recognised, and school curricula have changed, partly in response, the extent to which actual teaching styles and methods have evolved will vary from school to school and even from classroom to classroom. An individual teacher may be more innovative

Table 5.1 A comparison of pedagogies for the industrial and information societies

Aspect	Pedagogy in an industrial society	Pedagogy in the information society
Active learners	Activities prescribed by teacher Whole-class instruction Little variation in activities Pace determined by the programme	Activities determined by learners Small groups Many different activities Pace determined by learners
Collaborative	Individual Homogeneous groups Everyone for him/herself	Working in teams Heterogeneous groups Supporting each other
Creative	Reproductive learning Apply known solutions to problems	Productive learning Find new solutions to problems
Integrative	No link between theory and practice Separate subjects Discipline-based Individual teachers	Integrating theory and practice Relations between subjects Thematic Teams of teachers
Evaluative	Teacher-directed Summative	Student-directed Diagnostic

Source: After Voogt and Pelgrum (2005).

with some groups than others, for example when teaching those approaching an external assessment teachers tend to revert to more traditional, didactic methods. What has changed for everyone is that teachers are now working in a context where schools are encouraged to move from a traditional, mainstream, paper-based culture to one that is innovative and technology enabled, in effect from the bottom left to the top right of the axes shown in Figure 5.1.

In reality, although there is some evidence of innovation, most practice has moved across the bottom of this grid, from paper based to technology enabled, without noticeable innovation in pedagogy or outcome. The reasons for the reluctance of schools to innovate are many. Taking a more inquiry-based approach to teaching is challenging, and digital technologies can be disruptive (see Chapter 2). The benefits of such an approach are not always reflected in external assessment where coaching in content assimilation and test taking seem to be more effective. However, used well, inquiry-based pedagogies supported by digital technologies can be very powerful both to prepare for today's tests and examinations and to support learners in the world beyond school (see Magaña and Marzano, 2013 for an excellent review of research evidence and classroom practice).

Learning to solve problems

Applying knowledge and solving problems are elements of school curricula in many countries although managing the kinds of activity that offer opportunities to develop these skills in the classroom can be challenging for teachers. If

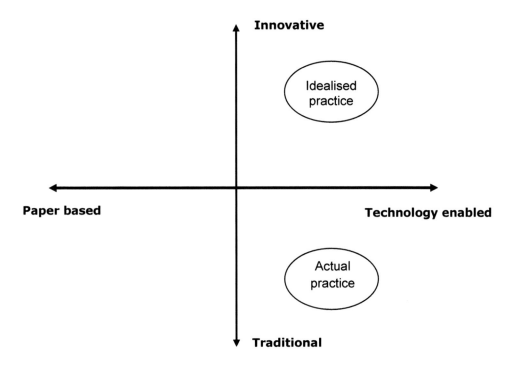

Figure 5.1 Axes of approaches to learning.

Source: Modified from McFarlane (2010).

learners are to tackle genuine problems in an open-ended way they will require a lot of help and support from the teacher as they set off in a variety of directions. The time taken by the task can be hard to judge and does not always conform to the timetabled slot. When working on an open-ended problem there are likely to be a number of possible dead ends. These can take time and become dispiriting. Finally, unless the learners take a role in formulating the problems they can become formulaic and fail to engage learners in the way necessary for meaningful learning.

Problem solving is a complex process that can be broken down into constituent parts, each of which requires particular skills which are both demanding and interrelated. These include:

- understanding and representing the problem, including identifying what kinds of information are relevant to its solution;
- gathering and organising relevant information;
- constructing and managing a plan of action or a strategy;
- reasoning, hypothesis-testing and decision-making;
- using various problem-solving tools.

(Whitebread, 1997, p. 17)

What is needed to help young learners experience these processes is a task or set of tasks that can support and scaffold exploration and trial and error in a context that has meaning, such as a narrative structure. It must also provide information in a way that provokes thinking and aids planning. Digital games can provide a starting point, offering information in a way that reveals resources as and when they are needed, or when a puzzle is solved, prompting actions and giving feedback to scaffold learning without intervention from the teacher. Such games also encourage trial and error, since, even though the result of the wrong choice may be that you get splatted, there is always the chance to have another go. Such an experience of failure can encourage a degree of advanced planning to avoid the same pitfall next time. Adventure games are particularly powerful formats for game-based problem solving as they present a series of smaller tasks within an overall narrative framework, usually some form of quest. They employ characters within the game that can inspire engagement and have levels that offer two advantages, they usually provide some inbuilt progression and they allow the game to be played in short bursts that suit the school context since the game position can be saved and the game restarted from a coherent point in the next session.

Educational software developers were quick to spot the potential of games to support learning. Hard-core games aficionados can be very scathing about such games, dismissing them as 'edutainment', and to be fair some of them are less than inspiring, being little more than multiple-choice questions with some pretty graphics, but there are many excellent titles that have stood the test of time in the classroom. Among these are adventure and exploration games that come with resources to aid the teacher to incorporate them into the curriculum. Some games designed for the leisure market can also support learning in the classroom with sufficient advanced preparation and a clear set of learning objectives (see Chapter 7).

Games can also provide an excellent starting point for learning collaboratively. Many games intended for use in schools may not be designed for use with more than one input device; however, small groups can easily gather around a shared screen to tackle problems together. The operational aspects of the game can also be shared, for example with one learner controlling the mouse, another reading out on-screen directions and a third keeping notes, changing roles from time to time. The fact that there is always a right answer, and possibly more than one, helps to referee disputes among the group as to the next action. In our survey of games use by teachers, we heard reports of children who found it difficult to negotiate in classroom contexts being helped by the fact that the computer game would demonstrate quickly whether they were right or wrong in a way they may not like but could not dispute. We also found that playing games with friends, and talking about the game play, were very common and spontaneous elements of game use in school and at home (McFarlane et al., 2002).

The strong context and narrative with clear characters can inspire work away from the computer. The development of artefacts based on the game such as maps or the use of a written record of activity, perhaps in the form of a mission log, can act as aids to the game play. At the same time these artefacts can support the planning and problem definition aspects of game-based problem solving by helping to work out where you are or what you did last time that ended in success or disaster (Whitebread, 1997).

Among the games specifically designed to support learning in a school context, one genre that has proved particularly successful and long-lived is based on the use of the LOGO programming language, popularised in the 1980s by its co-inventor Seymour Papert (1980). The game environment contains puzzles that give context to the use of turtle graphics, a form of LOGO where a string of commands is used to move a cursor on the screen and so draw a pattern. In these games the commands are often translated into regular English, selected from an on-screen tool bar, and used to create an image, for example to trace the elements of a bridge or wires of a circuit. This format frames the problem in such a way that all the commands needed are on screen and trial and error in their selection and the values used to determine angle and length of the lines drawn can be experimented with to work out the successful pattern. The context of the game gives meaning to the task, the software scaffolds learning through trial and error, and discussion among the group improves their chances of success. The scene is set for collaborative problem solving with little intervention from the teacher while the game is in play. The teacher's efforts can be directed to the setting up and debriefing elements of the lesson sequence.

The possibilities of programming

Programming computers as a subject for the school curriculum has gone in and out of fashion over the decades. Following the development of LOGO at the Massachusetts Institute of Technology (MIT) in the 1960s, the use of coding was at the heart of a movement advocating constructivist models of learning across schools and in particular in the primary phase (Papert, 1980). This simple yet powerful computer language was seen by some, including Papert, as offering an alternative to conventional schooling. Children were expected to learn to use it largely by trial and error and in so doing develop powerful problem solving skills which would equip them for life beyond LOGO. They would build programs to do whatever they needed from the computer. Indeed this assumption persists in some quarters and was part of the rationale behind the OLPC project. With strong associations with MIT, this project developed a purpose-built, low-cost machine designed for distribution in schools, particularly in the developing world. Some imagined that the children in receipt of these would write the programs they needed so the lack of software was not seen as a difficulty. In practice, as with every other educational technology, the actual impact of the ownership of these devices has not been quite as theorised, just as LOGO has not come to dominate the world's classrooms. While some learners take to the practice of coding with little coaching, most do need significant support, which most teachers cannot give without training. This is one reason that true LOGO only took hold as the main vehicle for learning in a small number of well-supported, experimental schools. However, one aspect of LOGO, turtle graphics, was used in primary classrooms very widely, largely in the context of mathematics or control technology where it was used to program various toys from small floor robots to complex Lego models.

Although it did not take over the world, LOGO still has its champions and followers as shown by the level of interest and quality of projects generated by the Scratch project. Scratch is a project of the Lifelong Kindergarten Group at the MIT Media Lab, which developed the software and made this available as a free download. Based on a LOGO-like language, Scratch allows users to program their own interactive stories, games and animations. The Scratch developers claim this process 'helps young people learn to think creatively, reason systematically, and work collaboratively – essential skills for life in the 21st century' (see http://scratch.mit. edu/). Certainly the array of over 4.5 million projects contributed is impressive and access to Scratch has given a global user base an outlet for their creativity. The topics for the productions are many and varied and come from every aspect of the school curriculum and well beyond. The Scratch group offers information on the website to support teachers and parents, which has no doubt helped adults to support a range of learners in school and at home.

In the UK LOGO is set for something of a renaissance, at least in the primary school. A revision to the statutory curriculum for England sees programming reappearing as part of a new subject called Computing, which also covers aspects of data and information handling previously within the subject called ICT. Some teachers, often now in positions of responsibility in schools, remember their days using LOGO, floor turtles and the LOGO family of games with fondness and are brushing off the dust and bringing them out once again.

Whether or not LOGO is the right language to use in schools, and there has always been a debate amongst computer scientists about that as it is unlike any language currently used to actually program computers, the re-introduction of programming is to be welcomed. There will be a need for support for teachers who do not have programming skills, but projects such as Scratch suggest this could be incorporated into online communities with some effect. There will surely be rewards in terms of the learning that is likely to result. Although the precise nature of the language used may not have relevance beyond the classroom – and if it is easy enough for even young children to use that will probably be the case – the process of programming will involve transferable skills. The need for precision, the inference of an internal logic, and the diagnostic fault finding needed when the code does something other than that intended, all help to develop rational calculative thinking. Programming, like adventure games, can provide an excellent context for developing problem solving as it too offers an intellectual sandbox, rather like learning Latin in days gone by. Unlike Latin exercises however, you get some feedback during the task and the resulting programs, especially within an environment such as *Scratch* or *The Crystal Rain Forest*, are more fun and accessible to most than *The Punic Wars*.

The challenge of inquiry-based tasks

Have you heard the one about the pupil engaged in a research-based project on the Renaissance who spent many happy hours surfing the internet, finding, collating and creating a presentation on Naples before anyone noticed the Naples in question was in Florida? This anecdote captures a widespread concern among teachers that learners will quickly go astray if set inquiry-based tasks outside a guided environment such as a game or a programming task. They will not be able to differentiate relevant information from the wealth of sources they find on the internet and as a result will waste a lot of time when pursuing open-ended tasks. Access to an infinite volume of information makes the ability to find and recognise exactly what you want more, not less, difficult (McFarlane and Roche, 2003). Search engines can appear to take the thought out of this process but are only as good as the queries used and the evaluation of the results they return. Schools have moved in a generation from a situation where the main sources of authoritative information were the text book in school and an encyclopaedia at home, to one where, at least at home, each learner will most likely have access to the web and will turn to a search engine as their first port of call.

Despite this change, models of learning that inform pedagogy are still predicated on assumptions of a body of common content to be assimilated by the learner. Statutory curricula have focused predominantly on a definition of the facts and figures to be taught and tested. It is still the case that school-level accreditation is given not for being good at History, Science, Mathematics, and so on, but for knowing about very specific topics in each subject and, usually, being able to reproduce particular interpretations or methods. The dominant model is still one where the uninitiated are inducted into a specified body of knowledge by a more expert other, in batches that are primarily based on the date of birth of the learner. It is hard to see much that is novel or innovative in the underlying paradigms of teacher and taught. Learning to create a meaningful websearch and evaluate and refine the results should be a mainstream cross-curricular activity, yet if it is taught explicitly at all it is usually confined to a lesson called IT or a relative of the same.

I want to look at a particular kind of generic open task that is commonplace, if not frequent, in most school systems, and the execution and learning outcomes when a more inquiry-based approach supported by particular digital tools is adopted within it. These tasks require the learner to produce content, which is most usually in the form of a written essay but could be a multimedia, video, audio or animated text. The pedagogical model I am looking at is a constructivist one, where the learner is invited to build a representation of their understanding of a narrative, explanation or description that might be fictional or factual in nature. The learner is likely to be using a range of sources to inform their own thinking but the purpose is to create a text that represents a view of what the learner knows, understands or believes on a given theme – ideally in response to a specific question or questions about that topic that frame the task and focus the activity.

This kind of task is not in itself new or original, or unique to the digital era. Setting learners a task that involves writing an account of a given subject they have researched in some way is a well-established practice in schools and probably has been since time immemorial. At least superficially, the way such tasks are carried out may look quite altered. Students will frequently use a word processor to produce an essay or construct a presentation using professional software, and use the internet – particularly sites such as Wikipedia – rather than pencil and paper and the family encyclopaedia.

So where is the problem? The task type remains valid – to create a text demonstrating familiarity with content – and the tools being used to do it are now relevant to the technology-rich culture the learners do and will inhabit. The end result is largely more visually impressive than the learners could produce with non-digital tools, not least because mistakes can be easily edited. But the nature of the end product and the process by which it is created is much the same as it has always been. This activity sits firmly in the bottom right corner of Figure 5.1 – using some technology-enabled techniques but in a very traditional framework.

The process of constructing the text is little changed, as it is assembled linearly with some editing but all too often a lot of straight cut and paste from the original source. The final version is little more than a first draft, produced by one individual, possibly with help from family if it was done at home. And yet this is against a background where those stakeholders who have a vested interest in the employment-ready state of students emerging from the education system seek learners with a range of skills that go beyond the tradition of individual essay writing. These include the ability to:

- find, evaluate, analyse and use information effectively
- communicate what they know effectively
- apply new and old knowledge to novel situations
- be flexible
- make decisions with an incomplete set of information
- work in a team.

(McFarlane, 2010, p. 154)

This skill set begins to represent the ways of knowledge building and application that are essential to an active and successful engagement with the knowledge society, where information is available in unprecedented volumes and collaborative working is the norm. Faced with unparalleled access to information and, critically, other people, via internet-based tools and content, this skill set becomes essential to building and communicating knowledge. How then might the practice of producing texts that document some familiarity with content be taken forward to become a collaborative, knowledge-building exercise?

Developing the iterative, creative task

Any task devised by a teacher, or a learner for that matter, to support learning will require some content, which may or may not be closely prescribed, and is likely to necessitate the use of some media or tools even if these are abstract as in a thinking exercise. There is also likely to be an implicit pedagogical model. The task itself then is formed at the overlap of content, media/tools and pedagogy (Figure 5.2).

Informed by the definition of knowledge-based pedagogy shown in Table 5.1, the task assumes a constructivist model of learning where the learner will be engaged in creating a representation of their own understanding through a productive task – writing, making a video or animation, and so on. The call for group work also means the task will include a social dimension. An extra element to the task design that is not mentioned by Voogt and Pelgrum but that I believe is

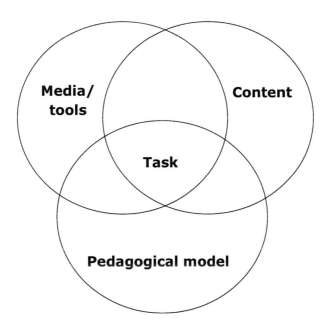

Figure 5.2 Components of a learning task.

Source: McFarlane (2010).

essential if analysis and reflection are to be meaningfully incorporated into learning tasks is iteration. In this iterative, productive model the learner does not work alone on the task, offering it for assessment to a teacher once complete. Rather she creates a number of drafts of the product, possibly working alone or with study partners, and at each stage offering the draft for comment and critique. This feedback may come from the teacher, other learners in the group or beyond, including family members. With each iteration she decides how and whether to respond to the input from others as she develops, clarifies, expands or otherwise edits her creation. This process of reflection and development may well be the most powerful element of the task in terms of skill and knowledge development (see Chapter 4).

Clearly there are a number of ways in which using digital tools makes this process of iteration and feedback much more accessible than with any use of pre-digital tools and materials. The malleability of all manner of digital texts makes the processes of drafting and editing much quicker and easier than any analogue equivalent. The ease of sharing also means others can view, comment and query. Although this can be achieved through the circulation of digital documents there are a number of tools designed so that more than one author can work directly on one text, simultaneously or asynchronously. Each contributor's input may be marked in a different colour and it is clear who exactly did or said what. The better learning platforms include such tools (see Chapter 4). The result is that this refinement and improvement of any piece of work becomes a natural part of the creative process rather than an onerous chore in the way that re-writing an essay by hand remains, for example (see Chapter 8).

So, we have a theoretical model of a learning task, constructivist in nature with a pedagogical model that is social and cultural, bringing in interaction with peers and experts, using digital tools that support an iterative process of content creation allowing for critical reflection and development prompted through interaction with members of one's learning community. In order for the model of the iterative, creative task theorised above to emerge, not only must there be meaningful and appropriate feedback from at least the teacher/tutor but also ideally the community to aid reflection, and the content created by the learner must be authentic. It must represent the actual world view of the author in a thoughtful way. That does not mean that every word or pixel has to be the original work of the author, indeed the appropriate incorporation of other sources should be encouraged to enrich the end result. Obviously, where content from other sources is used this must be done appropriately, that is without breaching copyright, and with full acknowledgement and accurate citation – skills that are not often taught at school level or not until post-16. The process of editing this content into a personal text is as much part of the creative act as the generation of the author's own content. Moreover, learners should be aware that this is an important and useful thing to do, an objective to be achieved largely by encouraging children to work with ideas and content that are relevant to and interest them and making the elements of the knowledge-building process, in particular the relevant conceptual artefacts, explicit. In this model of learning the process of education involves working with ideas to understand their nature, argue about and criticise them, and improve them. This echoes Scardamalia (2000) when she wrote: 'To work creatively students must become constructivists, and understand that knowledge is created and continually improved upon by people and that this is something they can do.' It is in this context of discussion and debate about the exact nature of the ideas being presented and explained where the real difference between writing an essay because a teacher has told you to and learning to be a self-reliant learner lies. Learners can engage with and benefit from such practices from an early age, establishing habits of thinking and working that they can hone and develop over time, taking more responsibility for their own learning as they go (McFarlane et al., 2000). However, teachers struggle to let go and hand that responsibility to learners particularly in a high-stakes testing environment. Certainly leaping straight into a fully developed model of inquiry-based and open-ended learning, expecting effective collaboration from the outset is likely to prove unsuccessful. Using a digital environment where some of the necessary skills can be developed in a guided yet challenging context can be a good place to start, and that is where digital games and programming tasks can be very useful in getting to grips with a collaborative, problem-based approach to learning and teaching.

A way forward

The learning model proposed here requires the development of problem-based tasks that pose genuine challenges. These present difficulties for classroom management that can be reduced through the use of a range of digital tools. Whether working in a game, designing a program or working on an entirely open task, reflection, feedback and development of ideas become a standard part of the process of learning. Moreover, that feedback can be provided by the software environment and the learners' active community of co-learners, not just the teacher. But we cannot assume that learners will naturally take to these ways of working, using the experiences they have acquired in the likes of Bebo and Facebook to acquire the skills and etiquette required to become successful collaborators or the problem-solving techniques they need through playing digital games. Effective collaboration and problem solving have to be learned, which probably means a combination of exposure to successful practitioners and some explicit teaching. Playing adventure games in school, working in a group, learning to program and working collaboratively to build authentic texts are all examples of activities than can be tackled through inquiry and support learners to build their skills in planning, testing ideas, trial and error and decision-making. However, these skills will only be developed and recognised as transferable where the design of the activity, the framing of the task and the reflection on it make this explicit. Using the digital tools that support a more active role for learners will only result in powerful knowledge construction if they are used to that end.

Summary

The emergence of the knowledge society calls for a re-think of what it means to be well educated. A contemporary debate seeks to set content knowledge against skill development, which I suggest is a sterile debate. While content knowledge remains important, it is also vital to know how to deal with new information and apply what is known in novel contexts. This chapter looks at the implications of this change for pedagogy and suggests how the use of adventure games, programming and inquiry-based tasks can be managed to help learners to develop valuable and transferable skills. Behind this model is a view of learning that is social and iterative. The skills needed to be a successful problem solver and knowledge builder will not spontaneously develop in all learners, and exposure to the tools and resources alone is not enough to guarantee success. The use of these powerful learning aids must be framed within meaningful tasks where the objectives and the processes of learning are made explicit, reflected upon and celebrated if a meaningful shift in pedagogy is to be effected.

References

Greenfield, S. (2004) *Tomorrow's People*. London: Penguin.

Lankshear, C., Peters, M. and Knobel, M. (2000) Information, knowledge and learning: Some issues facing epistemology and education in a digital age. *Journal of Philosophy of Education*, 34(1), pp. 17–39.

Lyotard, J.-F. (1984) *The Postmodern Condition: A Report on Knowledge*. Minneapolis: University of Minnesota Press.

McFarlane, A.E. (2010) Digital creativity – editing versus cheating and how you learn the difference, in Drotner, K. and Schrøder, K. (eds) *Digital Content Creation*. New York: Peter Lang (pp. 149–66).

McFarlane, A.E. and Roche, E. (2003) Kids and the Net: Constructing a view of the world. *Education, Communications and Information*, 3(1), pp. 151–7.

McFarlane, A.E., Bonnett, M.R. and Williams, J. (2000) Assessment and multimedia authoring – a technology for externalising understanding. *Journal of Computer Assisted Learning*, 16(3), pp. 201–12.

McFarlane, A.E., Sparrowhawk, A. and Heald, Y. (2002) The role of games in education. A research report to the DfES. http://teemeducation.org.uk/.

McFarlane, A.E., Triggs, P. and Yee, W.C. (2007) *Report on the Use of One to One Devices*. Coventry: Becta.

Magaña, S. and Marzano, R.J. (2013) *Enhancing the Art and Science of Teaching with Technology*. N.p.: Marzano Research Lab.

Papert, S. (1980) *Mindstorms: Children, Computers, and Powerful Ideas*. New York: Basic Books.

Scardamalia, M. (2000) Can schools enter a knowledge society? in Selinger, M. and Wynn, J. (eds) *Educational Technology and the Impact on Teaching and Learning*. Abingdon: Research Machines (pp. 5–9).

Voogt, J. and Pelgrum, H. (2005) ICT and curriculum change. *Human Technology*, 1(2), pp. 157–75.

Whitebread, D. (1997) Developing children's problem-solving, in McFarlane, A.E. (ed.) *IT and Authentic Learning – Realising the Potential of Computers in the Primary Classroom*. London: Routledge (pp. 13–37).

Chapter 6

User-generated content

The world of Web 2.0

The advent of Web 2.0 – where everyone has the potential to become an author as well as a reader of multimedia texts – enabled anyone with an internet connection to share products and creative acts with an audience. Before Web 2.0, communicating with a circle that stretched beyond your own personal contacts was beyond all but a selected elite. Broadcasting information to hundreds of thousands and even millions was the preserve of major corporations that owned cinemas, newspapers, magazines, radio or television channels. Those traditional channels remain central to mass media and the most successful have embraced web-based channels as part of their offer.

Media organisations have always needed and continue to employ specially trained people who can create and edit content, operate the sophisticated technology needed to produce that content and the means to distribute it. Those who develop content, edit and select it for distribution remain powerful and usually well-rewarded members of society. Their activities remain central to the mechanisms for information exchange, but their methods and approaches have evolved and continue to change as a result of the rise of audience involvement in the production and dissemination of what has become known as user-generated content (UGC). From photographs captured on a phone to carefully crafted films, a short response to a message board to a novel on a fan fiction site, a social software page to a personal blog, everyone with access to the internet can, in theory, join in the debate or start their own. Traditional media forms have embraced and integrated an audience using these new formats, for example by providing live reporting of user messages sent to a broadcaster in response to a featured item. All broadcast media now provide opportunities for comment and contribution in some form, and any organisation with a digital presence seeks user inputs. A 'two-screen' model of viewing broadcast TV is emerging where the audience members are using their smartphone or tablet at the same time as they watch a programme. New formats have emerged where the real-time interaction with the audience is incorporated into the programme, for example through voting or sending in content via a phone or tablet, which is used in the live broadcast.

New forms of information 'broadcasting' have emerged such as microblogging (pioneered by the popular platform Twitter) where users can send short texts, images and in some cases video or stop-frame animations. These are used by private individuals and public figures so that for the first time performers, politicians and pundits can address the public directly – or in some cases, their publicists can on their behalf. Celebrity users can address an audience of millions within seconds. These channels have a growing presence, are reported on in traditional media and offer users a route to a potentially global audience without resort to an intermediary. It is no longer necessary to master web editing software, which has in itself become easier to use and more widely available, or use a computer to post content on the internet. All you need is a phone and a microblogging account and it is as easy as sending a text message.

As members of the public find their own channels, no organisation or individual has control over messages about them; we all live in a commented world. Indeed the views of other users are taking precedence over anything produced by product or service providers themselves when it comes to monitoring or assessing the value and quality of a service or product. Digital reputation consists of the amalgamation of comments and reviews of those with personal experience to share and a new sector has grown up to service, or arguably create, this demand of which TripAdvisor, the travel review website, was a pioneering example.

Studying UGC practices

In this chapter I will look at the world of UCG and consider what is actually happening in terms of contribution and richness of content when young people take to this format to share their creative activity, and how the processes of commenting and review can contribute to the development of skills and knowledge. I will draw examples mainly from an Arts and Humanities Research Council-funded knowledge exchange project. This three-year study was a collaboration between the University of Bristol and the British Broadcasting Company (BBC). We looked at the activity around the BBC Blast project, which was designed to support and encourage young people to develop their creative skills in a range of media through online and offline engagement (Thornham and McFarlane, 2011).

The project provided rich examples of the potential and actual opportunities afforded by UGC practices across a wide range of media and gave us access to a large body of work and activity around the production and sharing of that work. Significantly, because we were able to continue the study over a three-year period, we gained insights into patterns of use over time, which is unusual. As well as conducting general surveys, we contacted and identified a range of participants to take part in interviews and analysed their contributions, of content and to message boards, in detail. Our research offered access to a cross-section of teenage demographic, levels of engagement with, and knowledge of, technology. We were able to survey and interview a population of young people who had engaged with BBC Blast and explore both their experience of Blast and their creative identities and activities more broadly. The population included users who had created and published content to produce a complex digital footprint that stretched from Facebook to YouTube and beyond. By mapping this footprint and interviewing creative practitioners, we were able to investigate conceptions and interpretations of their roles as producers and authors of texts. In conjunction with analyses of the texts themselves, and with the broader snapshot provided by the surveys, the research offered a triangulated investigation of creative identities in the broadest sense.

What emerged provides insights into the implications of this kind of out-of-school experience for productive tasks in the classroom and how the potential benefits might be harnessed to support and extend school-based learning.

BBC Blast and its users – a model of digital creativity

BBC Blast was designed to build capacity for creative practice in young people through engagement with online and offline interactions designed to support the development of their creative talents in seven areas: music, writing, art and design, fashion, computer games, film and dance. Registered online participants could post examples of their work and comment on the content posted by others. Mentors in each area monitored the posts and contributed from time to time. Face-to-face workshops run across the UK also offered hands-on activities in the different creative areas, but there was little overlap between those who attended the workshops and those who posted online.

We wanted to explore the profiles of users who post content, understand their creative activity within and beyond BBC Blast and gain some insight into non-participation as well as use. Data were collected via an online questionnaire and through interviews and analysis of the content posted in the discussions on message boards and the work posted on the various show case sites within BBC Blast. The questionnaire data did by definition represent the more frequent users of BBC Blast, that is the part of the population more likely to comment and offer feedback rather than peripheral users or observers. The interview data and the review of the content were more representative of the wider population of users and we used those to triangulate findings from the survey.

The survey data indicated 80 per cent of respondents were female, and that gender imbalance was also supported through the analysis of the logging activities, which found that, when actual names were offered, a much higher percentage of users were female than male. As to age, 44 per cent of respondents were in the 15–17 age category and 30 per cent were in the 13–15 age category. This suggests that the majority of contributors to BBC Blast are in the GCSE age group (also supported by the face-to-face workshop demographics and the mentor interview responses). Only 13 per cent of the respondents were in the 17–19 age category.

The results demonstrated a wide range of creative and technological competencies and interest within BBC Blast. It also became clear that teenagers do not upload content to a single website, nor do they upload all of the work they create.

How typical are BBC Blast users and their UGC habits?

In most respects, the use patterns we saw in BBC Blast do correspond to those emerging in reports from other large-scale research projects. The gender imbalance, with 80 per cent female is not unusual and may have implications for the behaviours of participants online. Sonia Livingstone's (2009) extensive work on teenage users of new media suggests particular trends are emerging specifically in relation to young female teenagers who are more likely to perform a supportive, friendly and enthusiastic identity online. Our data suggested that while females may be more likely to comment they were reluctant to post creative content on BBC Blast, which was reported in interviews as due to fear of negative reactions. This suggests a low level of confidence since negative comments on work on Blast were very unusual, in line with Livingstone's suggestion that social networking sites have a predominance of supportive comments and aligns with both the age and gender of the users. If it is the case that supportive roles are the norm for young female teenagers, yet they also fear negative reactions, then wider questions are raised about the possibility of generating the potential for critical dialogue that supports learning (see below) when, as in BBC Blast, 80 per cent of those who comment are female. It may be too simplistic to suggest that gender has a direct correlation with the level and nature of dialogue, but Livingstone's findings raise questions around how we encourage richer dialogue in a way that also negotiates gender performance online. It is noteworthy that these more positive behaviours are in stark contrast to those found in the cyberbullying research and suggest that the development of a sense of community online and personal identity within that community could mitigate some of the threats encountered elsewhere (see Chapter 3).

While it is easy to find examples of rich and complex UGC, there is also much that is trivial and that was the case with BBC Blast. Research into social networking sites has found that the quality and quantity of content posted depends as much on social and cultural factors as on website facilities (see Facer et al., 2003). In addition, web use is often conservative, and as Buckingham suggests, even banal: 'Most young people's everyday uses of the Internet are characterised not by spectacular forms of innovation and creativity, but by relatively mundane forms of communication and information retrieval' (2007, p. 14). Moreover, most users are passive rather than active. As Arthur (2006) suggests, it is only around 1 per cent of the user demographic that actually posts content. By comparison 10 per cent of the user demographic is likely to comment on the content, but the majority (89 per cent) is peripheral and rarely comments or produces content. This suggests that despite the technological facilities of Web 2.0, use continues to be primarily observational and insignificant in terms of content creation. Research into internet use by *young* people, however, does suggest that a significant number participate in some form of content-creating activities online (Crook and Harrison, 2008), although this does not mean the activity is prolonged or profound. Overall the patterns of contribution, comment and observation by BBC Blast users fitted within the norms seen in other, related research – most users restrict their activity to observation and short comments, a minority posts work of their own and a slightly larger proportion engages in discussion about work that goes beyond offering an opinion or asking a closed question.

Recognising learning dialogues

Although BBC Blast was not overtly designed as a social networking site, the message board and showcase facilities place BBC Blast within this genre. As well as offering space to post content, there is an open invitation to comment on others' work and engage in conversation around the work or related issues. The site was also designed with the intention of providing support for users to develop their creativity. So our research question was very much, can the interactions users experience around their posting of content actually support them to learn and to evidence this learning through development of their output? In order to explore these questions we analysed the dialogues that grew up around the content users posted to BBC Blast to see if they could be seen as learning dialogues, that is exchanges that can serve to support learning.

Wider research has found, as we did with BBC Blast, that much of the content of message board dialogues is trivial in terms of analysis or comment, rarely going beyond simple statements expressing admiration or possibly asking how the work was achieved and what tools were used. Although some positive reinforcement may well encourage further contribution, it is not going to provide much insight or provoke thinking to develop and refine the product in question. This raises the question of what a dialogue that does support learning might look like, as well as whether they are found in the kind of message boards that form part of sites such as BBC Blast.

Research into online learning practices has outlined a number of key behavioural indicators that contribute to an interaction between users with the potential to contribute to learning, a 'learning dialogue'. Learning dialogues can be characterised as social learning since they involve interaction between two or more individuals, and when conducted online they offer the opportunity for learnerto-learner interaction, for peer assistance and interaction with more experienced others acting officially or unofficially as mentors. Social learning can be thought of as an 'assisted performance' whether in relation to mentor assistance or peer assistance (Tharp and Gallimore, 1998; Ab-Jalil et al., 2004). This definition is useful because it encompasses the key behavioural indicators of learning dialogues, which are duration, reflection, alteration and iteration. These components of learning dialogues also resonate with Laurillard's (2002) work, which suggests that a learning dialogue includes discussion, interaction, adaption and reflection. Each of these accounts of learning dialogues foregrounds similar behaviours and it is worthwhile investigating these further.

Duration

As research into online learning environments demonstrates, the creation of social presence online through communication is vital in encouraging online social learning (Gunawardena, 1995; Tu, 2002, p. 38). By definition this requires sufficient contribution to an online dialogue to be meaningful, which may be expressed through the length, number, frequency and/or persistence of posting. Frequency increases the potential for rich dialogue not only because contributors return to read responses to their own posts, but they also return to further contribute to the debate. An increase in numbers of visits to a website also increases the level of dialogue as more people find the debates useful to them, and are therefore more likely to contribute in productive ways. The overall effect is a higher level of engagement and investment in the debate, which is not possible if contributors post once and never return. Indeed, as Tu (2002) suggests, social presence is a significant contributor to learning outcomes because the established level of debate or performance of the individual online has to be maintained, especially once social presence is established, that is, your group will miss you if you are absent for a period.

Reflection

Reflection is a key demonstrable outcome of a learning dialogue and can relate both to reflection of one's own opinion and reflection on other contributory points to the debate. As reflection demonstrates consideration, it is an important element of a learning dialogue and highlights exchanges where opinion has been thoughtfully considered and supported or debated. Reflection requires engagement and therefore a certain amount of longevity if the user considers their own point in relation to other comments or past experiences, so it is also linked to duration.

Alteration

Alteration tangibly evidences moments where opinion has been considered to a productive effect. In many ways, alteration is an outcome of reflection and consequently also requires duration. For alteration to occur, reconsideration must have been significant especially if it provokes the contributor to edit or change a piece of work as a consequence. It also evidences a judgement of value both on one's own original comment or work, and on the comments or criticism received about it. The process of alteration in response to comment in this informal context has much in common with improvement through formative assessment practices in the formal setting.

Iteration

As with reflection and alteration, iteration also requires longevity of engagement, that is, duration. Contributors must return to the conversation or debate in order to produce iterative dialogue. They must engage with previous comments or other people's work in order to contribute iteratively and productively. Iteration can also apply to the posted work itself, where subsequent versions altered in response to feedback are also posted.

Discussion

Discussion requires both duration and reflection as users demonstrate the ability to defend opinion and thought through discursive practice. They must engage in the language and techniques of that particular conversation, thus demonstrating longevity and commitment and continue to progress the debate through productive contributions and engage with and debate content posted by other users.

Interaction

Contributors must not only interact with other contributors, they must also interact with their previous comments. Interaction indicates a user is embedded in a shared practice as contributors demonstrate similar use of language and rhetoric. Interaction produces a sense of community and is clearly one of the aspects about the message boards that BBC Blast users appreciated. The collectively created fiction on the Writing Board, for example, demonstrates interaction at a highly productive level as users engage, contribute and produce new joint works.

Adaption

In a similar vein to alteration, adaption can be of an opinion or style of contribution. As users become more assimilated into the discourse of the website, they adapt language, style and rhetoric in conjunction with the other users. However, while adaption of language and rhetoric demonstrates a level of immersion or investment, the adaption of personal work to conform to the opinions and responses of others is important and arguably indicates an even greater level of commitment. Reflection, interaction, iteration and longevity are key contributory factors to adaption.

All the elements cited above describe a higher level of engagement and interaction than simple and singular posting to a message board. Although the elements may appear in varying degrees within each online conversation, they all require engagement in order to be productive. Singular posting (which the majority of contributions to the BBC Blast message board are) neither engage with previous comments, nor productively contribute. Instead, they tend to be statements of opinion or preference, and require no feedback or comment. The singular statements often close down discussion rather than invite it, and produce uninteresting dialogue for observers and peripheral contributors who are then less likely to respond. Taken together, the key contributory elements of learning describe a scenario where a user has become engaged, through duration and iteration, with a particular website or message board. She has learnt how to contribute through observation and discussion and then continued to return. In many ways, then, the key behavioural indicators also overlap with Lave and Wenger's (1991) notion of legitimate peripheral participation (LPP), which can be applied to the progression from 'newbie' to active user in online scenarios. Here, newcomers adjust to the affinity space (Gee, 2007) by initially observing and participating in minute and superficial, but important, ways. Through peripheral activities, users then become acquainted with the logistics and grammar of the website. Following observation, new users can model their own contributions on existing ones, and in time become core contributors. When the trajectory from newcomer to active user is demonstrated in this way, the detrimental effect of non-productive and disengaged comments or messages becomes apparent. If part of the impetus to contribute comes from observation, then reading closed statements of opinion or preference is less likely to encourage the observer to engage than reading a questioning or exploratory dialogue.

Can online creative communities support learning dialogues?

The research questions posed in our study of BBC Blast not only relate to whether the design and implementation of BBC Blast is conducive to learning dialogues, but they also relate to UGC sites more generally, and whether the discussions around, and comments on, content actually have the facility to support learning. From the analysis of the productive and learning dialogues in BBC Blast against Laurillard and Tharp and Gallimore's conceptions of learning conversations mentioned earlier, 17 per cent of the dialogue within the message boards emerges as productive or learning dialogues. The majority of discussions within the message boards are statements of opinion or preference that neither engage with previous comments, nor continue the discussion. Instead they close the dialogue down as they require neither response nor consideration from other message board members. The discussion below details responses to a query about favourite recent gigs. In what follows, the statements of activities and expressions of pleasure are straightforward responses to the original questions: they neither engage with the previous comment, nor do they ask any further questions. It is an example that demonstrates the content and tone of 83 per cent of the message board dialogue:

what's ya fav gig you've been to recently? what gigs are u looking forward to and what bands do you want to see?

I got cheap tickets to see Dolly Parton – she was fab!

Iron Maiden, Twickernham, 5th July. Oh my sweet lord it was awesome. I was on the pitch, damnit, it was so amazingly great.

Mcfly, M.E.N. Arena. With Elliot Minor. ☺ But I'm going to The Ting Tings very soon and R.E.M. in September, which should be good. I'd love to go to a The Verve gig, or Avril Lavigne

I went to GIAN (give it a name) not that long ago. It was awesome! Paramore, Plain white t's, you me at six, to name but a few.

None of the key behavioural characteristics of learning dialogues outlined above (duration, reflection, alteration, discussion, interaction and adaption) are evidenced above as users simply post non-related comments in response to the original question. The dialogue is much more focused on establishing similarities of experience rather than actually debating or discussing the various gigs. Indeed, it is akin to Livingstone's findings of dialogue on social networking sites, which works to align contributors of the discussion into similar opinions or activities (2009). The overall aim of these discussions is to produce supportive and friendly, non-threatening environments. The similarities in terms of the design and tone of the message board community by comparison with social networking sites seem to be producing similar performances within both environments. This has a lot in common with the first step in Salmon's (2000) hierarchy of interaction where activity serves to induct members into a social group before any meaningful dialogue to support learning can take place.

Where message board activity related directly to the content posted by users, the Writing and Music boards, for example, where actual content can be posted along with comments and criticism, we found a much higher percentage of learning dialogues. Learning conversations are also much more likely with loyal and returning users to a particular board. It was clearly the case that productive contributions within the message boards were the outcomes of a few key users. Contributors to one particular message board (rather than to a range of boards) have a higher percentage of contributions to learning dialogues. This suggests that there is a consistency of performance within the boards, and those consistently offering good feedback continue to do so. The following excerpt is from a discussion in response to a song lyric posted by a frequent contributor to the music section:

I'm thinking very fast punk. Or perhaps some American-sounding indie? Great song, by the way!

I LOVE this. Please don't take this at all the wrong way if I say that it reminds me of an updated 'I Want'-type Disney song. It has all the hope and promise – and none of the schmaltz – fab.

I really really like this. I think it needs to be upbeat and girly – and with a really powerful bassline. Sexy too, I think.

I quite like this – but for some reason not QUITE as much as I normally enjoy your work. I'm trying to work out why and I'm wondering whether some of the words feel a little as though they have been put in because they rhyme rather than because they are the best word for the job. 'Numb' is the one that sticks in my head mostly and 'hoping they'll get the message through.' In fact reading it again I'm wondering if it's ONLY the chorus that I'm not wild about. It's not bad – none of your stuff is – and with the right tune it may work very well. I guess it's just not my favourite of your songs.

I really like this. My favourite line is 'I'm not a loud person, not many people know that'.

If learning dialogues are produced through contributions from a key group of people who consistently offer good feedback, then high-quality responses need to be established from the start. Modelling answers and offering tools for constructive criticism are therefore key to establishing good dialogue within the message boards, especially as this will compel the more peripheral users (the browsers) to offer good quality responses when/if they do begin to comment. The BBC Blast 'Writing' messageboard, which has a much higher percentage of learning dialogue by comparison with the other boards, not only lends itself to a learning exchange in terms of design (as creative work can be posted alongside, and chronologically related to, the feedback), but it also has a core group of consistent users, including the writing host (mentor), who model answers and offer good feedback. This raises the level of dialogue within the board more generally and means that anyone seeking the techniques and tools to comment (through observation) can assess the level at which they are required to respond.

Although learning discussions are much rarer than the more chatty threads within the boards, the statistic of 17 per cent is quite high by comparison with social networking sites. However, when the productive dialogues are compared with other writing-based websites such as www.fanfiction.net, where learning dialogues not only emerge *without* intervention of a mentor but also start at a grass roots level, the dialogues are much less advanced in Blast, especially in terms of analyses of the created content (Cheng and McFarlane, 2006). This suggests not only that some UGC formats lend themselves more readily to the development of learning dialogues via message boards, but it also emphasises that it is primarily a core, loyal and interested group of users who are necessary for productive exchange. The dialogues on websites such as fanfiction.net are between returning users with a commitment to the activity on the site, which increases the potential for iterative and reflective exchange.

Is lurking desirable?

Lave and Wenger's (1991) notion of situated learning, and especially their conception of LPP, goes some way towards theorising the browsers of BBC Blast and positioning them at least within the possibility of productive learning exchanges. LPP is useful for the analysis of online use because it is also accounts for how newcomers to websites, for example, can become more involved users. Legitimate peripheral participation also works in conjunction with James Gee's (2003) notion of an 'affinity space'. Affinity space, as Gee argues, replaces connotations of togetherness, communication and societal relations implied by a 'community', with those of a common goal and organisation based on interaction rather than external or top-down logics. Moreover, people may come together in an affinity space for a common purpose that can be fleeting or long-lived, or a mix of both for different users. Within affinity spaces, the shape and look of the texts produced depend on an affinity of logic, which, in turn, is generated by the users themselves. Seen in this light, LPP outlines the process of alignment to the affinity space through an initial learning of the logics of the space, which then translates into a production and support of them. LPP offers a more positive account of the browsers or 'lurkers' on the website. The theory suggests that rather than simply observing, 'lurkers' are actually learning the logistics of the space and this may be an important stage before some will eventually contribute in more tangibly and visibly productive ways. LPP also suggests that membership of a community of practice, or an affinity space, is mediated by the possible forms of participation. If newcomers can directly observe the practices of core users, mentors and experts, they can understand the broader context into which their own efforts fit. Finally, then, LPP widens possible participatory groups for the website beyond the 1 per cent of users who do actually consistently post content.

What does it mean to be an active user?

The final issue of UGC online relates to a wider social and cultural issue about what it *means* to be perceived as an active user. The online questionnaire data from BBC Blast suggest more than half of the respondents who are already (by virtue of their active response) considered more committed and active users, continue to perceive themselves primarily as *browsers* or infrequent users of the website. This raises questions about how important or relevant it is to avoid the label of an active online participant. Furthermore, if actively posting content (or admitting to it) is not perceived as socially acceptable activity, then there are implications for a website that relies on UGC. The implicit assumption of BBC Blast is not only that teenagers want to, and do, create content, but there is also an implicit assumption that they want to discuss their creation and gain recognition for it. It is worth remembering Livingstone's assertions that '[y]oung people's lives are increasingly mediated by information and communication technologies, yet their use of these technologies depends in turn on the social and cultural contexts of their daily lives' (2002, p. 30).

Expectations of interest in UGC seem tied to the myth of the digital native, for whom the politics or visibility of uploading content is not perceived as an issue, indeed rarely even considered. If it is the case that users are conscious of and sceptical about being labelled as an active contributor to a website (Thornham and McFarlane, 2011), then the question of successful UGC as a foundational model for websites or other media to support learning comes under scrutiny. This issue also seems compounded by research into young people and new media and the unhelpful creation of a hegemonic active group of teenagers and young people who post content. As Buckingham argues, before any research can be undertaken in relation to young people and new media, 'we need to jettison any essentialist assumptions about the differences between children and adults' (2006, p. 11). Age may in fact not be a factor in determining the likelihood of an individual becoming an active member of an online creative community. Certainly youth is not a guarantee of active participation or facility with the practice.

UGC in a school context

The findings from research into UGC practices of young people so far suggest several pointers for those wishing to consider the use of learning dialogues centring on media generation as a vehicle for learning. First, it is helpful to get a sense of learners' current levels of activity and interest in UGC and to expect this to be varied. Some, perhaps most, will have little or no previous experience, while there may be a few committed users. The relevance and value of participation may need to be explained, and some users will need support to engage with the format even if it is within an established school learning platform.

The most productive scenarios involve dialogues around content and, where this often departs from broader VLE use, that content should have been produced by the group. The format of the content may vary, the text could be written, visual, audio or video. Some thought should be given as to how comment will be recorded – will this be as comments or tracked changes within a text, a separate commentary, comments on a message board or an alternative edit, for example of a video clip. The task should be designed to be iterative in nature with an assumption that drafts/versions will be posted for comment prior to revision and re-posting informed by the comments received. This will mean that there must be enough time allocated for the task. Additionally, the expectations and etiquette around commenting and feedback will need to be established.

Learning how to comment and how to engage in dialogue around the development of content does not come naturally to everyone, but can be learned through peripheral participation. It is perfectly acceptable to start off by browsing and experiencing the norms of the environment. For that reason, it helps to have identified an existing community as an exemplar. Once the practice is established, this could be a group of more experienced users within the school. If the activity is entirely new, it may help to find an existing online community such as a fan fiction site to review and critique as a model for a site the group members set up for themselves. It is also important to model the kinds of contribution you are hoping to see – these should be open ended, inviting reflection and adaption. A common challenge with the input from BBC Blast mentors was that they tended to give closed responses to work or comments from users, which were seen as the final word from the 'expert' and had the effect of closing down any further discussion.

Finally, posting work for critical review is a scary process for many users. A code of conduct should be negotiated so that comments are helpful even when pointing out deficiencies. Before asking learners to expose their work to the whole class, it may be better to begin with contributions that are produced by small groups, and/or creating smaller units that review one another before opening out to the whole class or even beyond. Developing a culture of learning through dialogue will take time, but there is evidence that it can reap rewards. It will give a purpose to each learner's work as they will have an audience, moreover an audience that will give them feedback. Feedback is a vital part of formative assessment without which it can be difficult to improve performance. Teachers are unlikely to have time to give the volume of feedback a learning set can provide, or to look at more than one draft for large numbers of students. Harnessing the critical faculties of the whole group increases the capacity for reflection and adaption and everyone benefits. Editing and reviewing are both valuable learning activities, and seeing examples of work that is better or worse than your own creates a better sense of what improvement looks like.

Although the research base stems largely from users over the age of 12, there are examples of schools that are using this approach earlier. By using a closed-school system any issues relating to the minimum age for UGC site subscriptions are avoided. It seems it is never too early to begin induction into the world of UGC communities as a vehicle for reflective learning. The benefits are likely to be life-long and to provide an excellent basis for participation in a contributory digital world.

Summary

Web 2.0, where users can comment on content and create and post content of their own, is now well established and the social media that have grown up as a result of this functionality are changing publishing and broadcasting. This chapter reports on a study of young people's engagement with a purpose-built Web 2.0 space designed to foster creativity across a range of media through the sharing of creative content made by users and discussion of their work, as well as the wider world of those media, via moderated discussion boards. The study examined the extent to which the resulting practices of participants could be said to be supporting learning, and whether these behaviours could be said to be representative of Web 2.0 activity more widely. The characteristics of learning conversations as used to analyse the content of message boards are set out, with evidence that such conversations, although in a minority, do arise in this informal learning context. The participants and their behaviours as captured in this project, BBC Blast, are compared to statistics on wider use of online media by young people as an indicator of how much we can safely extrapolate from this research. The experiences of active contributors and those who take a more observational role are taken into account. The implications of the experience of engagement with UGC for school-based learning are then considered.

References

Ab-Jalil, H., McFarlane, A., Md. Yunus, M. and Mohd. Saufi, M. (2004) Assistance in electronic discussions. Proceeding of the fifth International Conference on Information Communication Technologies in Education.

Arthur, C. (2006) What is the 1% rule? *The Guardian*, 20 July. www.theguardian.com/technology/2006/jul/20/guardianweeklytechnologysection2.

Buckingham, D. (2006) The electronic generation? Children and new media in Lievrouw, L.A. and Livingstone, S. (eds) *The Handbook of New Media*. London: Sage (pp. 77–89).

Buckingham, D. (ed.) (2007) *Youth, Identity and Digital Media*. Cambridge, MA: The MIT Press.

Cheng, C. and McFarlane, A. (2006) Gaming culture and digital literacy: Inspiration and audience. *Nordic Journal of Digital Literacy*, 02(1), pp. 91–105.

Crook, C. and Harrison, C. (2008) *Web 2.0 Technologies for Learning at Key Stages 3 and 4*. Coventry: Becta.

Facer, K., Furlong, J., Furlong, R. and Sutherland, R. (2003) *ScreenPlay: Children and Computing in the Home*. London: RoutledgeFalmer.

Gee, J.P. (2003) *What Video Games Have to Teach Us about Learning and Literacy*. New York: Palgrave Macmillan.

Gee, J.P. (2007) *Good Video Games and Good Learning: Collected Essays on Video Games, Learning, and Literacy*. New York: Peter Lang

Gunawardena, C.N. (1995) Social presence theory and implications for interaction and collaborative learning in computer conferences. *International Journal of Educational Telecommunications*, 1(2/3), pp. 147–66.

Laurillard, L. (2002) *Rethinking University Teaching: A Conversational Framework for the Effective Use of Learning Technologies*. Second edition. London: RoutledgeFalmer.

Lave, J. and Wenger, E. (1991) *Situated Learning: Legitimate Peripheral Participation*. Cambridge: Cambridge University Press.

Livingstone, S. (2002) *Young People and New Media*. London: Sage.

Livingstone, S. (2009) *Children and the Internet*. Cambridge: Polity Press.

Salmon, G. (2000) *E-moderating: The Key to Teaching and Learning Online*. London: Kogan Page.

Tharp, R.G. and Gallimore, R. (1998) *Rousing Minds to Life*. Cambridge: Cambridge University Press.

Thornham, H. and McFarlane, A. (2011) Discourses of the digital native: Use, non-use, and perceptions of use in BBC Blast. *Information, Communication and Society*, 14(2), pp. 258–79.

Tu, C.-H. (2002) The measurement of social presence in an online learning environment. *International Journal on E-Learning*, April–June, pp. 34–45.

Chapter 7

Games and play

Fun for all

Computer and video games arouse strong passions. The compulsive, some would say addictive, nature of the player experience, the controversial content of some genres and the perception of gaming as a solitary experience all combine to show digital gaming in a challenging light.[1] Many commentators, especially in the popular media, are ready to associate digital game play with anti-social behaviour at best and criminal violence and pornography at worst. This is to miss the rich variety and complexity of the digital gaming world. Indeed there are games that many would condemn as violent or in other ways explicitly unpleasant, for example by reinforcing unwelcome racial or gender stereotypes. Similarly there are cinema and television entertainment offerings that are inappropriate for young viewers. For this reason, cinema releases are given appropriate age ratings and certain broadcasts are scheduled late in the evening. It is also why digital games carry age ratings, similar to those used for film, and some games are rated as over-18, that is, adult. Interestingly, however, families are not always as sensitive to these ratings as they are to those for film and TV (Sanger, 1997). Perhaps because they are 'games', there is an assumption that they must be suitable for the young, which is to overlook the growing market for adult games. Indeed the global, digital gaming market, when hardware purchases are included, has surpassed that for film in terms of value and probably customers and the big spenders are adults. Adult gamers are not restricted to the under-30s and one of the fastest growing market segments is women over 50, which is counter to two popular preconceptions about games and gamers. The archetype gamer is not a teenage male alone in his darkened room, pale skinned and febrile as he shoots aliens. He or she is just as likely to be a middle-aged adult playing a word game with family members online.

The playing of digital games is now an established cultural practice for millions of individuals of all ages. The range of digital games available is large and varied, from online poker to simple puzzle games, from arcade-style shooting galleries to virtual worlds where hundreds of thousands of people interact in real time in a fantasy context. It is thus very difficult to make any meaningful general comments about digital games or game play. It is unusual to find a child, even in less developed countries, with no knowledge of digital games, even though this knowledge may not be derived from personal play experiences (Williamson and Facer, 2004). Many, though not all, children appear to enjoy such games and to engage with them for considerable periods of time (Somekh et al., 2002; McFarlane et al., 2002). Such play is also widely recognised as related to a range of forms of learning, many of which have importance beyond the context of the game (Gee, 2003; Becker, 2006). It is, however, the level of engagement with digital games that has evoked the interest of educators, and there is a resulting belief that if such engagement could be harnessed for learning relevant to the formal education agenda a positive impact on the outcomes of schooling could be achieved (for a discussion of this see Kirriemuir and McFarlane, 2004). Indeed there has been a small number of important projects looking at the development of games specifically to support education (Sandford et al., 2006; Rudd, 2013). However, there is still little published research in the area of effectiveness of digital games to support learning, and it is very difficult to make any kind of meaningful meta-analysis of what there is. One reason for this difficulty is that digital games themselves are far from uniform in character and therefore in potential impact. Moreover we lack a coherent vocabulary to describe the character of such games in a way that is meaningful in terms of learning. Most reports on learning in games are happy to describe a game according to the broad categories used to market them, and offer little or no title-specific information. Thus we find on the same conference programme the effects of immersion in a complex 3D world on information gathering next to the effect on hotel receptionist training of a series of multiple-choice questions on static screens depicting an exchange with a potential guest, both described as 'games'. This situation is further complicated by the fact that many of those attempting to use research on games to inform policy or practice in education may have only a passing familiarity with gaming.

What is a game?

It is revealing that even though games studies is an established discipline, and game design is one of the fastest-growing subjects for new courses in universities, there is not yet one, undisputed definition of a game, whether digital or otherwise. Clearly a game involves some form of structured play, where play is an activity that is usually voluntary, intrinsically motivating, involves some level of engagement and has a make-believe element (Blanchard and Cheska, 1985; Rieber, 1996; Yawkey and Pellegrini, 1984). In a range of discussions on this topic, most authors agree on at least two common elements; a game must have at least one player, and there are rules of play. Avedon and Sutton-Smith (1971, p. 7) in their landmark book *The Study of Games* suggest that a game is 'an exercise of voluntary control systems in which there is an opposition between forces, confined by a procedure and rules in order to produce a disequilibrial outcome'. Clearly for these authors a game must have a winner. Indeed most games are competitive, and have a goal or goals within them although the competition may be entirely self-directed, with the player aiming to beat herself or triumph over the game or its designer. Most games also use resources of some kind, even if these are intangible such as memory or actions of another player.

The model developed by Jan Klabbers (1996) defines the game as a system in which an actor or actors interact with each other and resources via a set of rules. A common feature of digital games, however, is that unlike many traditional games where the rules are explicit and usually made known to all before play commences, the majority of digital games reveal the means to succeed through the actions, and responses to the actions, of the players as they play. For example, in conventional chess a would-be player who does not know the rules, left alone with a chess set, is free to move a piece in any direction on the board, never learning anything of the rules of chess. In contrast, in the digital representation of the game of chess the algorithms for each piece are coded so the player can only move the pieces legally. As a result, given time and systematic trial and error, it would be possible to infer the rule governing each piece in a way that is impossible using physical pieces and a board alone. The digital game environment is designed to support such inferential learning at a pace and in a style that ensures enough players will persist and succeed to make the game commercially viable. As Kücklich (2003) points out, it is not that the player necessarily elicits the rules of the game in this process, but they learn how to react in order to survive in the game.

In his book on the relationship between learning and digital games James Paul Gee (2003) sets out 36 principles of learning that can be found in games. Katrin Becker (2006) offers an analysis of learning within games in terms of nine well-established models of learning and learning style, from Gagné to Gardner, and makes a convincing case that whatever the preferred guru of pedagogy, there is a digital game to suit every approach. What remains contentious is the degree to which such learning is relevant and transferable to contexts beyond gaming. Authors such as Gee (2003) and Jenkins (2000) make strong cases for the relevance of such game literacy to wider competence in a multimodal, connected world. In formal education generally, however, there remain concerns as to the applicability of such learning, in terms of content as well as context, and the debate on the precise nature of the relationship between game play and education, especially in institutions such as schools and universities, remains active (Kirriemuir and McFarlane, 2004; Rudd, 2013). What emerges from the debate is that, as with any use of technology to support learning, access to the tool alone is not enough, and the wider context and framing of the play is essential to effect meaningful learning. Also there should be a match between the experiences offered in the game and the intended learning outcomes whether they are related to exposition of content, exposure to process or practice of skills.

Categorising games

In a study of commercial off-the-shelf games in the classroom (McFarlane et al., 2002), we used a simple commercial categorisation to ensure that the games used were representative of the market (Table 7.1). This categorisation emphasises the nature of the player experience, not surprisingly as it is primarily a marketing tool to help potential purchasers understand what they might expect from playing the game. Although adequate for the aforementioned study, this classification has little power in a wider context not least since many games cross the boundaries of the genres used, and there is wide variation in complexity and quality within each genre.

Starting from a different perspective, Will Wright, designer of *SimCity*, argues that current computer games might be divided into the following three categories according to the activities unfolding through game playing: contests, hobbies and interactive stories (Figure 7.1). In contest games competition, winning and losing are the key elements. *Unreal Tournament*, *Madden Football* and *Quake* are typical examples of such games. In hobby games players build characters or scenarios

Table 7.1 The genres of commercial off-the-shelf games used in the TEEM report

Genres of title	Key features of genre
Adventures/ quests	The adventures offer a series of challenges usually within an overarching scenario. The tasks in the game may be relevant to the school curriculum.
Simulations	The player operates a model/simulation that then behaves according to a pre-programmed set of rules, which may match those in the school curriculum, or those in real life, or may be fantastic.
Race games	The player operates a vehicle around an obstacle course. It may be possible to configure the course and/or the vehicles in which case this becomes a special case of simulation.
Maze games	Movement in 3D or 2D space, with obstacles to overcome/challenges to meet. Timing is critical, heavy reliance on motor skills, memory and planning.
Edutainment activities	Activities structured with a view of loosely supporting education, usually a combination of activities and games with an overtly educational intent. Can range from skill development, e.g. hand–eye coordination, concentration, memory, problem solving or creation of an outcome based on the content provided – video, picture, subset of an art package including product specific clip art or stamps, video library, music clips and some basic skills materials as well.
Creative/model building	This is often a component of the game rather than the game in itself. For example, some of the race titles involve creating a course, or building the car before you can race it.
Shooting/arcade games	By aiming and firing at objects, which are usually moving, they are destroyed. This involves the development of fast hand–eye coordination.

McFarlane et al. (2002).

Figure 7.1 Wright's (2001) typology of contemporary computer games after Squire (2004).

while playing games. Then they publish them on the web to share with other hobbyists. *SimCity* is a very popular computer game falling into this category. Finally, there are interactive story games, where the game experience is about participating in an interactive story, such as in *Final Fantasy X* or *Baldur's Gate*. Wright also acknowledges that there are overlaps in this classification. Take *Civilization* for example. It seems that it should be placed somewhere between contests and hobbies (Wright, 2001).

Wright's model could be said to put clear ground between the complex and involving style of game to which the work of authors such as Gee and Jenkins refers, and the type of game that is commonly found in work on games and learning that are much simpler in scope. Examples include the titles commonly grouped as edutainment titles and training games. These commonly use drill and practice routines, with no characterisation and interaction limited to selections from scripted alternatives. The simplest of these are built on a set of multiple-choice options; even though they may be dressed up with attractive animations, sounds, videos, and so on, the player is still choosing from a fixed set of options. Such software is not regarded as a true game by those immersed in complex game design or research. They cannot 'offer the player the opportunity to engage with a dynamic system from an experiential perspective . . . provided by the freedom to interact with, and have control over a simulated system' (Woods, 2004). However, when interviewing children using mathematics drill and practice software as part of a research project on one-to-one device use (see Chapter 2), it was clear that they regarded these applications as games and spoke about 'playing' them, which underlines that the players' perception of the 'play' is a major component in deciding what actually constitutes a game.

The need for a model

The absence of a clear model for defining games represents a challenge to an educator who wants to look holistically at the potential of digital games to support learning. This problem is akin to that facing those engaged in researching educational software more broadly. Large-scale projects looking for the effects of either educational technology or games are unlikely to be entirely successful since neither educational technology nor games offer a single homogeneous variable (see, for example, the problems in interpretation arising in the major ImpaCT2 study (Harrison et al., 2002)). We are left in both cases trying to interpret research findings where we are invited to view an adventure game, or a simulation game, or a talking book as if those genres represented a variable of constant value. In other words, we are invited to assume one study using an example of one of these genres can be compared with another with some degree of reliability. The reality, of course, is that not only will the way in which the software is used affect any outcomes, but also variations between the software titles within a genre will also impact. A simple example comes from the study of a science simulation where a failure to frame the task meant that, even with an accurate simulation of the genetics of cat breeding, learners failed to grasp the role of probability in the outcomes, but did find the graphic representation of each litter an aid to pattern recognition (McFarlane and Sakellariou, 2002). Clearly how successful such an intervention is deemed to be depends on the context and the prevailing objectives of the teaching. However, even if these issues are dealt with through adequate description of context and objective, the problem of failure to adequately differentiate the software tool remains.

Clearly a common framework for analysis of the software tool would be helpful. Simply to resort to rich descriptions of the title will not satisfy the information gap, and would take too long. Moreover, it is currently unclear which features should be described and, without a common frame of reference, it is still unlikely that studies could be compared. A small number of models to map the important aspects of a title have emerged from the game design community, and these do help to illuminate the complexity.

Modelling games

Much of the work attempting to define and model games comes from the fields of game studies and game design. Some relate only to digital games and others attempt to be more general in their scope. Klabbers (2009, for a summary of a range of earlier work) identified that all games can be rendered into three components: actors, rules and resources, and the interactions between them. Subsequently a number of authors have attempted to offer models of games, and although they may not use his terms, or even reference Klabbers, they all recognise these three components. Indeed much writing about digital games and digital gaming is remarkable not least for the almost complete lack of cross-reference to the body of work looking at games, play and learning more broadly, which is perhaps a mark of an immature domain.

The detail in the different models comes in the sub-categorisation of each of the three components – actors, rules and resources – and the nature of the interactions or interfaces between them. The Game Object Model (GOM) of Amory (2001), is unusual in that it takes account of the potential for learning and proposes to map the key elements of a simulation adventure game designed for education in an attempt to 'formalize the relationship between educational theory, game design, play and development' (p. 251). His variables are:

- Game space: play, exploration, challenges, engagement.
- Visualisation space: story line, critical thinking, discovery, goal formation, goal completion, competition, practice.
- Elements: fun, graphics, sound, technology.
- Actor/s: drama, interaction, gestures.
- Problems: manipulation, memory, logic, mathematics, reflexes.

Amory looks at space in terms of play, exploration, engagement and challenge, all of which depend on the player not just the designed options. Echoing Marshev and Popov (1983), Amory is interested in how you play. Klabbers (2009) also looks at the player and the role of motivation, why you play. This player perspective is powerful since in evaluation of the relationship between game play and learning, for both digital and conventional games, an important factor determining the learning outcome is the quality of the set up – that is, why and how you play – and the post-game de-briefing session where the players reflect on their experience, draw out their learning and give it context. As with other educational technology, it is as much the way the resource is used as the design of the resource that determines how effective it is at supporting learning.

Using design models to deconstruct COTS games

A question remains as to whether or not the models used to analyse or design games, or predict the combinations of elements that could be used to build games, can be used to deconstruct the functionality of commercial games in relation to learning, and thus offer comparable definitions of these games and their potential for supporting learning, and the nature of the learning that might result from playing.

GOM places learning objectives at the start of the design process and all else follows from this. In analysing a game that is already built, it is necessary to work backwards to infer the learning objectives, which may or may not have been intended within the original vision of the game or may be incidental to game play. Moreover, in the design model the look and feel are related to the design of puzzles, which is in turn related directly to the learning objectives and intended to reinforce 'core concepts'. Amory et al. (1999) claim that GOM 'allowed educational philosophies to be closely allied with the development of the game and provided a framework for story and interactive puzzle creation'.

But there is a question as to whether any of these models are adequate to describe a game as a process, which is perhaps where the potential for learning is at its most powerful since, as Friedman (1995) notes, you can interact with a process and learn about it. There are also problems of creating complexity akin to the real world in a game – can we offer an embodied experience of the world as seen by a 'professional' in that context e.g. as a biologist, or a designer, or an accountant or a journalist? Could we produce a microworld as complex as the epistemic game environment of Shaffer's work (Shaffer, 2008)? Is the purpose of a game to give the player experience of an epistemic frame, or at least a subset of it? Crawford (1982, p. 8) describes simulations as 'a serious attempt to accurately represent a real phenomenon' while a game is 'an artistically simplified representation of a phenomenon' suggesting that games do not intend to represent reality. If so, surely it is clear that it is only by a comparative analysis of the experience of the game and the real world that the player/learner can clearly differentiate what has been learned of reality and what remains fantasy.

The conclusion seems to be that although there are models that could inform the design of a game to support learning, these are not particularly helpful when faced with a commercial game to assess for its potential in the curriculum. Each game must be considered individually, and the context of the game play will be as important as the actual play in determining the possible learning outcomes.

Games are easy, right?

Anyone who has attempted to master a complex digital game, or even play for more than a few minutes, will know that these games are not easy. They take hours of practice and require a degree of resilience to master. Indeed the development of resilience may be one of the desirable by-products of game play (Gee, 2003). But in terms of the development of declarative knowledge or transferable skills, it makes a difference why the game is demanding. Difficulty may be operational, not content related, for example discovering and then performing complex actions such as jumping and turning in mid-air using a key combination it is difficult to perform so that practice is required to perfect the technique. Crawford (1982) differentiates between skill and action games and strategy games. The latter are characterised by the use of in-game challenges.

These can require complex problem-solving strategies that go beyond trial and error and offer a powerful sandbox in which to learn and practice problem-solving skills. It is this type of game that opens up particularly rich possibilities in the classroom.

Using complex problem-solving games to support learning

To illustrate how game play can support learning in a range of contexts I want to draw on a project that offered teachers from schools in south-west England and India an opportunity to work together to explore how they might use games to support a more inquiry-based approach to teaching and learning. The Unbox 21 project (http://unbox21.org/bc/) was supported by the British Council and its website contains research reports from the UK's Futurelab, which are very helpful for anyone interested in trying to use games in the classroom.

I particularly want to refer to the work with *Machinarium*, which was chosen as one of the packages by teachers in the project. It has many advantages: it offers an adventure game format that involves a range of challenges based on elements of the physical science curriculum; it is web-based and so will run on a range of computer types; the language component is small – it is a very visual experience – which is helpful for an international project; and the first levels can be accessed for free. Perhaps most important of all, it also offers an excellent game experience and is great fun to play.

An interesting aspect to this project, and one that sets it apart, is that the researchers and teachers adopted a framework of learning objectives to inform the design of teaching interventions using the games. This was based on the Leap 21 framework from SRI International and ITL Research and documented the learning activity objectives against three dimensions: collaboration, knowledge building and use of ICT to support learning. Each of these dimensions was chosen as it is widely recognised in definitions of twenty-first-century learning skills, that is those needed to underpin an authentic learning experience in a digital world (see Chapter 1). To aid differentiation and ensure read across of the different learning experiences, each dimension is broken down into four stages so that each activity can be defined at one of the four stages on each of the three dimensions. Clearly in order to be able accurately to describe an activity on this framework the teachers needed to be very familiar with the game and the activities they would use to complement game play draw out and reinforce learning. The time permitted to each participating teacher to work with colleagues to gain this first-hand experience and knowledge of the software and to plan related activities within the learning objectives framework was critical to the success of the project. In this case this extended to visits to each other's countries, which certainly enriched the project and was important to explore the cultural portability of this approach but is clearly not essential to the adoption of the model more widely.

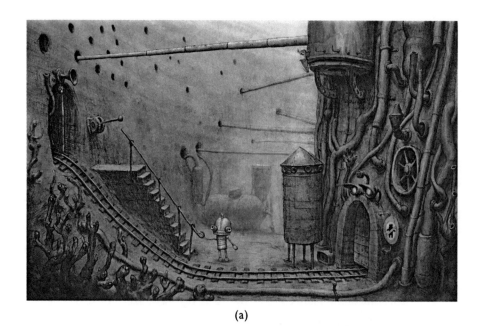

(a)

(b)

Figure 7.2 (a) A screenshot from *Machinarium* shows the robot facing a complex mechanical and logic problem. (b) The thought bubble in the inset image shows the visual nature of prompts offered.

The research report offers evidence of learning in all the three dimensions and the project shows that the use of an engaging game can be a powerful stimulus for change in the classroom. Through working collaboratively to analyse the game, develop activities and document their plans and the outcomes using a simple yet powerful common framework, the teachers in the Unbox 21 project were able to move their pedagogy along the spectrum from didactic to inquiry-based. The focus of the lessons expanded beyond familiarity with content to include defined skill development. The challenge-based design of the game supported learners to take a problem-solving approach to their learning, which they found both fun and satisfying. Activities were undertaken by groups and in some cases whole classes using a shared screen through a data projector thus offering opportunities for collaborative learning. The game provided inspiration for a series of spin-off activities from designing additional levels of the game with new science challenges to composing animations of phenomena such as a demonstration of forces using figures and apparatus made with modelling clay. These activities acted to draw out and reinforce in-game learning. Teachers reported improvements in a range of skills:

> These included team-working, collaboration, co-operation, creativity, critical thinking, problem solving, logical thinking, strategy, information sharing and analysis skills. Many also felt pupils were developing a language and keener appreciation of such skills and why they were important, with some teachers stating pupils had become more resourceful, responsible and resilient as a result.
>
> (Rudd, 2013, p. 5)

This project, in common with many other technology-based interventions, relies on teacher report for its evidence of impact on learning and in many spheres this is not given a great deal of weight. Unfortunately the kind of skill development the teachers believe to have occurred is not captured in many standardised tests. In the case of Unbox 21, this was not the intention – but in terms of evaluating the overall impact of games in the classroom, as with any other technology-based intervention, policy makers require proof that goes beyond the opinion of the trained educators who work with students over an extended period.

This constant tension, between learning that is evidenced through changes in test results and learning evidenced through teacher assessment is one that has dogged the development of technology use in the classroom. Is any reported difference in learning real? Valuable? Important but different from that captured in the tests? Different and not important? These questions continue to echo through the debates between researchers, policy makers and educators as to the nature of authentic learning with technology and we are no closer it seems to answering them. But until we do it will remain difficult, if not impossible, to be clear about the real value of game-based learning, or any other kind.

Summary

Digital games are a popular and growing part of the contemporary leisure land-scape for adults and children. Defining a game, any game, digital or otherwise, is not straightforward, even though most people recognise one when they see it. Modelling the elements of a game can help to inform the likelihood of a game supporting learning at the design stage but inferring that potential from a com-mercial game is not straightforward. Complex problem-solving games can offer rich potential in the classroom and act as a vehicle for changing teacher practice to make it more oriented to inquiry-based learning. A study developed with teachers in India and the UK shows that, with the right framework and common protocols to work to, game-based learning can cross cultural boundaries and result in highly effective outcomes for teachers and learners.

Note

1 The industry distinguishes between computer and video games since they are aimed at different hardware platforms: the personal computer versus some form of games console. However, in this chapter that distinction is not an important one and from this point the term 'digital games' will be used to include any game that runs on a microprocessor-based system, in contrast to a game that does not involve such a digital device.

References

Amory, A. (2001) Building an educational adventure game: Theory, design, and lessons. *Journal of Interactive Learning Research*, 12 (2/3), pp. 249–63.
Amory, A., Naicker, J.V. and Adams, C. (1999) The use of computer games as an educational tool: Identification of appropriate game types and game elements. *British Journal of Educational Technology*, 30(4), pp. 311–21.
Avedon, E.M. and Sutton-Smith, B. (1971) *The Study of Games*. New York: Wiley.
Becker, K. (2006) Pedagogy in commercial video games, in Gibson, D., Aldrich, C. and Prensky, M. (eds) *Games and Simulations in Online Learning: Research and Development Frameworks*. N.p.: Idea Group Inc. www.idea-group.com/.
Blanchard, K. and Cheska, A. (1985) *The Anthropology of Sport: An Introduction*. S. Hadley, MA: Bergin & Garvey Publisher, Inc.
Crawford, C. (1982) *The Art of Computer Game Design*. Out of print: available online at www-rohan.sdsu.edu/~stewart/cs583/ACGD_ArtComputerGameDesign_ChrisCrawford_1982.pdf.
Friedman, T. (1995) Making sense of software, in Jones, S. (ed.) *CyberSociety: Computer Mediated Communication and Community*. Thousand Oaks, CA: Sage (pp. 73–89).
Gee, J.P. (2003) *What Video Games Have to Teach Us about Learning and Literacy*. New York: Palgrave Macmillan.
Harrison, C., Comber, C., Fisher, T., Haw, K., Lewin, C. et al. (2002) *ImpaCT2 – The Impact of Information and Communications Technology on Pupil Learning and Attainment*. London: Becta/DfES.

Jenkins, H. (2000) Art form for the digital age – Video games shape our culture. It's time we took them seriously. *Technology Review*, 103(5), p. 117.

Kirriemuir, J. and McFarlane, A. (2004) A literature review on computer games and learning. Report 7. Nesta Futurelab, Bristol. www.nestafuturelab.org.

Klabbers, J. (1996) Problem framing through gaming: Learning to manage complexity, uncertainty and value adjustment. *Journal Simulation & Gaming*, 27(1), pp. 74–91.

Klabbers, J. (2009) *The Magic Circle: Principles of Gaming and Simulation*. Third and revised edition. Rotterdam: SensePublishers.

Kücklich, J. (2003) Perspectives of computer games philology. *Games Studies: International Journal of Computer Game Research*, 3(1).

McFarlane, A. and Sakellariou, S. (2002) The role of ICT in science education. *Cambridge Journal of Education*, 32(2), pp. 219–32.

McFarlane, A., Sparrowhawk, A. and Heald, Y. (2002) The role of games in education. A research report to the DfES. http://teemeducation.org.uk/.

Marshev, V. and Popov, A. (1983) Elements of a theory of gaming, in Ståhl, I. (ed.) *Operational Gaming*. Oxford: Pergamon Press (pp. 53–9).

Rieber, L.P. (1996) Animation as feedback in a computer-based simulation: Representation matters. *Educational Technology Research & Development*, 44(1), pp. 5–22.

Rudd, T. (2013) *Commercial Off-the-shelf Digital Games in the Classroom: The First Steps*. British Council Unbox21 Project Research Report. www.britishcouncil.in.

Sandford, R., Ulicsak, M., Facer, K. and Rudd, T. (2006) *Teaching with Games: Using Commercial Off-the-shelf Computer Games in Formal Education*. London: Futurelab. www2.futurelab.org.uk/resources/documents/project_reports/teaching_with_games/TWG_report.pdf.

Sanger, J. (ed.) (1997) *Young Children, Videos and Computer Games: Issues for Teachers and Parent*. London: Falmer Press.

Shaffer, D.W. (2008) *How Computer Games Help Children Learn*. New York: Palgrave Macmillan.

Somekh, B., Lewin, C., Mavers, D., Fisher, T., Harrison, C. et al. (2002) *ImpaCT2 – Pupils' and Teachers' Perceptions of ICT in the Home, School and Community*. London: Becta/DfES.

Squire, K.D. (2004) Replaying history: Learning world history through playing *Civilization III*. PhD thesis, Indiana University.

Williamson, B. and Facer, K. (2004) More than 'just a game': The implications for schools of children's computer games communities. *Education, Communication and Information*, 4 (2/3), pp. 255–70.

Wright, W. (2001) Design Plunder Keynote at the 2001 Gaming Developers Conference, CA.

Woods, S. (2004) Loading the dice: The challenge of serious videogames. *Game Studies: International Journal of Computer Game Research*, 4(1).

Yawkey, T.D. and Pellegrini, A.D. (eds) (1984) *Child's Play: Developmental and Applied*. Hillsdale, NJ: Lawrence Erlbaum Associates.

Chapter 8

Thinking about writing

Standards in literacy

International comparisons of educational performance coordinated by the OECD offer league tables comparing results from tests in reading, maths and science taken by thousands of students in over 60 education systems every three years. These PISA results are always given significant media coverage, with relative positions and particularly changes of position prominently reported. It is surely the case, certainly in democratic systems, that this reporting influences thinking and policy, particularly when a country slips in the ratings. There is much debate among educational researchers about the precise validity of these comparisons, but politicians give every appearance of taking them very seriously. It is very noticeable that Anglophone countries, by and large, have been slipping or static in the ratings. This also chimes with the internal political rhetoric in the UK and US that standards in basic education have not been improving. A further OECD study in 2013 (OECD, 2013a) was widely reported in the media as showing that, for the first time, school leavers in the UK were less literate that those retiring from the workforce although in fact the data is open to other interpretations – but despite significant investment in implementing various policies aimed at driving up standards, the test improvements were not achieved (OECD, 2013b). The predominant political view of education in the English-speaking world is that standards are at best static and students leave school without the necessary skills in basic numeracy, literacy and digital technologies they need to be economically active members of society. And this matters since, as the foreword to the OECD report points out:

> The median hourly wage of workers who can make complex inferences and evaluate subtle truth claims or arguments in written texts is more than 60 per cent higher than for workers who can, at best, read relatively short texts to locate a single piece of information.
>
> (OECD, 2013a, p. 26)

Arguably this whole book addresses the question of what it means to be literate in the first part of the twenty-first century and takes an expanded view of literacy to include a wide range of competences with digital information. Indeed the PISA exercise in 2012 included a test of problem solving in a computer-based environment to reflect the changing requirements of education. Competence with digital technologies of various kinds is dealt with elsewhere in this volume but here I want to look at literacy in a more traditional sense; that, is the ability to create and decode texts and, in particular, strings of words in order to communicate meaning. Facility with text is arguably more, not less, important in a digital context as exposure to complex, multimedia formats requires sophisticated decoding skills and an ability to work with the written word. In particular I want to look at writing as a component of literacy and how that has changed and is changing in a digital context.

At one point in the late 1990s and early 2000s word processing was the dominant use of computers in schools (Somekh et al., 2002). Most learners only experienced this for very short periods of time as ratios of learners to computers rarely exceeded 18:1. It was not uncommon for the exercise to focus on learning to operate the device, typically by typing out a text written by hand for the purpose of producing a neat copy, possibly for display. This was a very different experience of digital text from that of the present-day owner of at least one and probably more devices that allow them to generate text digitally, where that text may vary from a 140-character communication to a full essay or lab report. Here I will look at some of the implications of that change for writing in relation to school-based learning.

Working with digital text

The role of the word processor

Digital text creation is so integrated into our use of digital devices that we rarely use the term word processor any more. Like desktop publishing before it, the term has lost currency as software packages become more powerful, with greater functionality and the number of dedicated packages we need for general use is reduced. Not only can we do more with each individual device we use, we can generally do more with each software application on a personal computer. Arguably, with the advent of 'apps' on smartphones and tablets, that trend is now reversed – but in terms of so-called 'productivity tools' such as text-processing and data-manipulation packages it remains true (see also Chapter 9 on data handling).

The potential of the word processor to enhance learning in schools, particularly in the context of the language curriculum, has been widely praised for several decades. As early as 1988 *The Kingman Report* indicated that the word processor can have widespread implications for the way children write:

> The word processor, with its ability to shape, delete and move text around provides the means by which pupils can achieve a satisfactory product. . . .

Through the use of word processors pupils are drawn into explicit discussion of the nature and likely impact of what they write. They will begin to talk about appropriate structure, correct punctuation and spelling and the vocabulary appropriate for their audience.

(DES, 1988, p. 37, section 4.13)

At the time that report was written this potential was largely a matter for speculation rather than the result of consideration of evidence (Adams, 1990). On the basis of perceived value and potential, the use of word processing was embedded in the National Curriculum for the UK from its first iteration and this was also the case more broadly, for example in the state curricula in the US and the IT MasterPlan in Singapore. Perhaps it is not surprising then that, even as late as 1995, data collected by the Ministry of Education in the UK showed that over 50 per cent of school use of computers was for word processing. This only changed in the first decade of the twenty-first century when internet access became widespread in schools and the most common use of computers, outside lessons specifically to teach how to use the technology, was to find information on the web and use it to create digital slide presentations.

It is interesting that given access to an expensive and relatively scarce resource in schools – where one-to-one access is far from the norm in any country – teachers still choose to set tasks that use computers to create a neat presentation of information. Is it that this is indeed the most valuable use of digital devices to support learning, or is it that these are the uses with which teachers themselves are most familiar and so feel more comfortable to supervise? Or worse, is it that these tasks are ones the learners can get on with on their own with little need for supervision? In a review of research into group work at the computer Eraut and Hoyles (1988), quoted in McMahon (1990, pp. 157–8), commented that 'assigning pupils to work on computers allows the teacher to attend to the rest of the class in peace'. McMahon further commented that the choice of software might depend 'more on its capacity to keep pupils busily occupied than on the learning gains it might promote'.

The popularity of word processing, or the use of presentation software to create texts, might owe much to the wishful thinking of educationalists and policy makers and the degree to which creating such texts keeps learners absorbed. In some classrooms this may still be the case but there is evidence that the potential is indeed far greater and that this potential can be harnessed. Kuhn and Stannard's review of the use of computers in the English curriculum as long ago as 1996 still offers useful insights into the use of text manipulation in the development of writing. What has changed since that time is that more learners will have access to devices for enough time to make their use effective. Only now are we seeing access levels reaching the point where the potential of device use can be transformed into meaningful learning as the tasks accomplished could be of sufficient frequency and duration. Moreover, increased access could mean the results of small-scale pilots are finally scalable to the mainstream classroom. However, access alone it not enough – spending more time on tasks designed primarily to keep you busy is unlikely to impact on broader learning outcomes. For that, the task itself has to be re-thought, but before that we also have to look at effective use of the device.

The ergonomics of using the keyboard

There was a time, in living memory, when schools offered lessons in keyboard skills. Secondary-school students spent time learning to use a QWERTY keyboard without looking at the keys, using all ten digits, reading what they were writing instead of looking for the next letter. With practice it was common to be able to type 60–100 words a minute. However, not everyone was given the chance to acquire this very useful skill. Predominantly these lucky learners were female and not in the top sets. These were the young people earmarked for the typing pool – an historic facility common in businesses of any size until the advent of the personal computer, when email took over and responsibility for producing business communications became dispersed throughout the workforce.

This association of typing skill with a technical education aimed at the less highly achieving student is important, as it led to reluctance, if not hostility, towards the teaching of all learners, from an early age, to type efficiently. Amid predictions that the QWERTY keyboard was soon to be obsolete, during the heyday of investment and hype around computer use in schools in the 1990s and early 2000s the very idea that children should be drilled in typing was heresy. But the QWERTY layout remains even where it is present on a smartphone or tablet screen. We have a whole generation of learners who use QWERTY keyboards all the time, with many errors, and achieve very low input times. Clever algorithms such as those used in predictive text and auto-correction packages help, spell checking and grammar support make a difference too. But surely not being able to touch type is the digital equivalent of never having been shown how to hold a pen correctly or form letters legibly on the page? Any lengthy writing is likely to be done via a keyboard you could touch type on if you knew how. Even the most avid SMS (text) user is unlikely to prefer to write an essay with their thumbs.

So I continue to advocate access to a touch typing tutorial for all learners from an early age so that they learn to use the keyboard without thinking, can produce accurate output quickly and efficiently and get on with the thinking and writing. This does not have to take up valuable time in school as the software can be used at home. There may well be concerns in relation to stress injury linked to repeated use of keyboard and pointer; getting the ergonomics of the work station right should be part of the course. Sitting on your bed with a laptop in your lap is one of the favoured positions for home use by young people – and it seems likely to lead to various postural problems.

The nature of the writing task

And what of the matter of the task? Once everyone has access to a screen there really is no reason why origination of content cannot be done digitally. The older practices of only working at the screen in pairs or larger groups should not be abandoned since this practice, originally born of necessity, has many benefits that are well recognised (Crook, 1994). Indeed, working to a shared screen is in many ways a powerful context for social and collaborative learning in both the face-to-face and at-a-distance contexts. However, once there is sufficient time to work on screen there really is little reason to restrict use to the older established practices of keying in first drafts written on paper and using the editing facilities only to correct errors, neaten the presentation and correct the punctuation.

The Impact 3 study of the classroom practices in 2010 found that in ICT-rich classroom environments the use of computers had moved on (Crook et al., 2010). Now it seems the dominant activity is searching for content and then producing slide shows in presentation software. Clearly the devil here is in the detail. It is all too easy for such tasks to degenerate to a cut and paste exercise with little evidence of comprehension or analysis of the content being used. The result may appear as a coherent set of slides, but this format is not conducive to the development of a narrative or subtle or nuanced arguments.

It would appear that the aspiration for text editing expressed in *The Kingman Report* (DES, 1988) is not yet the established norm in most classrooms. The use of a text editor as a tool to develop arguments, refine ideas and clarify thinking is not part of the everyday experience of writing in school. The practices that are now so well established in professional and academic writing and that have revolutionised the publishing industry are all but absent. The lost opportunity is thrown into stark relief when the importance of writing as a tool for learning as expressed by Jessel is considered:

> Being able to capture and represent our thoughts in the form of written text and have them available for further scrutiny is an important ingredient in thinking and learning. Text can convey ideas and the recording of text allows ideas to be re-read and reflected upon. . . . If we wish children to work in this way it is important to encourage them to view writing as a mutable entity, something to be experimented with in the process of their learning.
>
> (Jessel, 1992, p. 23)

So the importance of developing the habit of viewing text as something to be considered, evaluated and revisited is not an issue restricted to the composition of stories, nor is it simply about creating error-free copy in terms of spelling, punctuation and grammar, or a text that is decorative for presentation. Rather it is a fundamental facet of the learning process, where text becomes a tool through which we make tangible our thoughts as we develop and hone them into a coherent narrative, which makes sense first of all to ourselves and then to others. Indeed this perspective puts the creation of text at the heart of the development of thinking itself. Shared texts are fundamental to the development of rationality. Before the development of texts in the evolution of humans, and before a child learns to access text, the mind has only current experience and what can be remembered as the raw material for thought. The development of text facilitated reflective, abstract thought and the communication of those thoughts to others. This realisation has profound implications for the way a teacher views the use of text in the process of learning and the importance of reading and writing (Bonnett, 1994). The teacher and the learner in a digital context have access to tools that allow for the creation and manipulation of text quickly and easily. This goes beyond the process of simply coding and decoding a written text and developing familiarity with the protocols of spelling, grammar and punctuation, which is what conventional literacy can become. With access to word processors the objectives of writing to impact on learning must surely align with those skills and attitudes valued by Jessel (1992) and which Egan includes under the notion of 'comprehensive literacy' (Egan, 1990).

Sadly, access to word processors has not in fact expanded the emphasis of teaching and learning beyond conventional literacy, and this is largely what is being measured in the international comparisons and where it seems progress at raising standards is somewhat stalled at best. Despite the widespread use of electronic text, which makes the otherwise intensely laborious process of drafting, editing and experimenting with text accessible to even the youngest scholar, most written exercises in school rarely progress beyond a first draft and even that may never be completed. Use of word processing is still in danger of remaining in the ghetto of computing lessons with a focus on technical mastery, or if the objectives do go further they may only apply within that subject and not extend to the use of text across the curriculum as a powerful tool to support the development of thinking. Worse, the view of electronic text in a school setting is often negative since the ways children and young people use these most commonly, for short message formats, have developed a grammar and syntax of their own. Whether you see this as a creative and innovative development of language or an appalling degradation in standards of literacy is largely a matter of perspective. One thing is apparent, however, which is that when such use of language strays into the realm of the more formal settings of school and particularly the examination room, it is likely to disadvantage the writer. The fact that this happens, and examiners' reports suggest it is a common problem, seems to me an indication that we have not adapted our teaching of literacy even at the basic level to suit a digital generation since we are not teaching them how to nuance their use of language for different contexts and audiences and the likely consequences of getting this wrong.

Developing writing

It seems that there can be no guarantee that the use of word processors in itself will result in the hoped-for developments in children's writing as we have known for some time (see Peacock and Breese, 1990). Indeed there is a body of evidence that suggests that the key to releasing the potential promise of the word processor, as with any other learning scenario, is effective teacher intervention. I therefore wish to look now at the process of creating, reviewing and developing texts and the kind of tasks teachers can design and the interventions they can offer to assist the development of 'comprehensive literacy'. There are many reasons that learners create texts. Much of the writing students do in school from an early age is to create a record of a task or to describe a narrative, which may be fictional or factual such as the record of a field trip or a science investigation. It is important to note that what follows is not restricted to conventional literacy or technology elements of the curriculum, and much of it is not restricted to the development of texts that are solely composed of words.

Making a mark

In order to create some kind of personal record or statement, it is necessary to create a mark. That has traditionally started with pictures and letters formed on a surface by hand and we encourage children to start this from a very early age, long before they have the motor control needed to do it accurately. Such activity is an important part of development of a range of skills, not least hand–eye coordination, and I am certainly not arguing for any reduction in such activity in the early years curriculum. However, when we want to start using these skills to get children to create texts for wider learning purposes it may be more effective to introduce other tools, less demanding of precise motor control or physical strength alongside the conventional. It is not uncommon for young children to use cameras to capture images rather than draw, and alternative input devices that allow children to create texts before they master the QWERTY keyboard have been common in schools for many years before the touchscreen made them redundant. Progress to mastery of the QWERTY keyboard eventually is desirable, as I have argued above, but is not essential for early use. Moreover, onscreen keyboards on devices such as tablets do away with any concerns that young writers may find dealing with a capitalised keyboard difficult when hunting for letters they only recognise in lower case – at the tap of a finger they can move between the two with ease. Indeed, touchscreen use can also support the development of writing by hand as software that offers exercises to form letters and words on the screen and give feedback on performance can be used.

There are thus many ways in which a digital device can be used to assist children in forming letters, and subsequently words on screen, that can also support the development of hand writing. As their writing develops, children may spend longer on the development of a text and write more when they use a text processor (Peacock, 1993). No one familiar with young writers can be unaware of the sheer physical effort it takes to form letters on a page, and this only diminishes slightly for many older children and young people. The views of Maria, aged 9/10, that 'the keyboard doesn't ache your hand' will surely resonate with many young and not so young writers (Jessel, 1992, p. 26). It is unlikely in the early stages that any one child will be writing long enough to be at risk of repetitive strain injury but I refer back to the earlier section on the importance of learning to use digital writing tools correctly to lessen this risk as writing develops.

In our longitudinal study of young learners with one-to-one devices over two to three years it was always a puzzle to me that no-one thought to work with them on the use of the various aids to text creation they had at their disposal. Many picked this up for themselves or more commonly where shown by a family member or friend, but many did not, yet again showing that physical access to technology alone is not enough for the potential it offers to support learning to be realised. For example, spell checkers, or predictive text, may help to improve spelling but only if they are used correctly. These aids will often accept a synonym or auto-complete with an entirely different word so care and some understanding are needed to use them effectively. Learners with severe problems with letter order may not be helped at all by these tools as they may be unable to distinguish between the alternatives offered to them.

Composition

Where the word processor is used purely as an amanuensis to help produce a fair copy, or the digital camera is used indiscriminately to capture endless still or moving images, the true power of the technology to support learning is clearly severely under-exploited. The real power of these digital-text creation tools is the flexibility they offer. When working on paper or with analogue media generally, learners are usually left with a final version that in any other context would be a first edit, perhaps with some comments from the teacher taken into account. A text in electronic format is infinitely mutable. It can be revisited, changed, expanded or cut as needed to produce an end result the author is happy with, and that perhaps better reflects the ideas she has developed in her head.

The potential to make corrections easily without leaving evidence of a change, which mars the appearance of a physical copy, was recognised as an important aspect of digital editing as part of learning from the early 1990s (Stradling et al., 1994, p. 20). Copying out a piece of work by hand, especially more than once, is rarely pleasurable. Indeed the thought that copying out may be required can be a real brake on creativity: 'I write less, then I have less to copy' (quoted in Loveless, 1995, p. 27). The facility for changing text with a word processor need not obliterate the stages of development that a text has undergone, however. Print outs of each iteration can be made if necessary for assessment and profiling purposes. Digital storage and retrieval is more efficient but version control is vital when copies are stored electronically (see Chapter 4). These versions have the advantage that changes can be tracked and the author of each element can be logged. This can be very powerful when the end result is a piece of collaborative composition. Reviewing earlier versions can also help the learner and the teacher recognise progress. Having earlier work available to review was a key facility used and appreciated by learners who had use of one-to-one devices in our longitudinal study (see Chapter 2).

There is evidence from observations of young writers using word processors that despite the possibility and ease of drafting and redrafting it is unlikely that the majority of learners will begin to do this spontaneously. When Crook observed pairs of children working together to write stories using a word processor, it was evident that the story grew sentence by sentence. The children discussed the composition of each sentence and the narrative content within it. However, they rarely re-read more that the last sentence of the story, although previous events were mentioned in discussions relating to what could happen next (Crook, 1994). Similarly, Jessel (1992) reports that pairs of children given a writing task where the final sentence of the story was agreed at the beginning, as an encouragement to plan a narrative, still composed sentence by sentence. Any spontaneous redrafting at the end was restricted to correcting spelling and punctuation. Changes to the narrative were only evoked by questions from the observer. Crook's and Jessel's observations confirm that the opportunity to compose must consist of more than simply time at the screen if there is to be deep engagement with the process of editing and the quality of the final product. Young writers do not progress naturally to taking a broader view of the whole piece before they begin or as they write. Nor do they spontaneously go back and redraft what they write without prompting.

The teacher can encourage the development of a more sophisticated approach to creating a text through judicious questioning and guided discussion or by structuring a task so that it involves discrete elements of planning, creation and editing, combined in a reflective and iterative pattern. Working collaboratively can also help to hone the outputs of the various stages and working together on a screen can deepen a sense of shared ownership of the product as everyone can see a large screen and the keyboard can be passed between the group members. Again the fact that alterations can be made easily as the work develops helps to facilitate the refining of the final plan. It is also easier for the teacher to see the work in progress as she monitors the groups and to intervene to ask questions or make suggestions based on the shared text.

The planning stage is important for all formats but is especially so for those that involve images or sound where there is a possibility of simply pressing the record button and capturing a lot of material indiscriminately, thus expanding the analysis and editing phase to such an extent that it becomes impractical. One strategy for ensuring that each step is taken in turn and given some thought is to build in a peer-review element. Groups of students can 'pitch' their ideas to another group at the planning stage using a story board. The reviewers can question the structure, motivations, evidence base, rationale, and so on, and could be provided with a set of evaluation questions to score against, giving a rationale in each case. Such questioning can help sharpen thinking and focus attention on detail for both the authors and critics.

In order to develop the perspective that work created by students is something to reflect on and revisit, it is important to make it clear from the outset that this will be the case and indeed for this to be the norm rather than an exception in the curriculum. Where the prevalent practice is to only work on a given piece of text creation in one sitting, which may not even be completed or looked at by the teacher, let alone re-visited, and where a piece of work is only revisited to make corrections if it is really poor rather than to develop ideas, initial reactions to redrafting may be negative. 'Having to do it again' may be viewed as censure rather than an exciting opportunity to develop ideas. Making the overall shape of the task explicit at the outset may help, with reminders as the work unfolds. This is perhaps something we do not do enough in the classroom. As a result learners do not develop a sense of the process as a whole, and the point of the different stages, even if they do have experience of the constituent elements.

It is important to point out at this stage that a significant aspect of becoming a developed and experienced author is the ability to make informed choices regarding the medium used for a particular purpose. The word processor may well be the first choice of many adult writers for most of the time, and that can be true for some young writers. Others may prefer to use images, or to work with a more free-form layout than digital tools will easily support. In order to make informed choices it is important that learners have experience of a range of media and methods and, moreover, that they learn to make critical judgements of each. Media studies has become a derided term in the UK, but some understanding of the power and pitfalls of different media formats is surely an important element of genuine literacy in a world where we are surrounded by so many forms of rich media. It is also important to remain critical of work produced in various media as we would be with a written text. Too often I have seen teachers lavishly praise work that is actually quite mundane because it has been produced in a format that is quite sophisticated. Use of video and animation can be particularly difficult as we generally lack a 'grammar' of these media and can be overly impressed by technical competence at the expense of effective narrative or accurate communication. In innovative lessons where learners have been given the choice of the medium used to summarise their learning in mathematics I have seen very effective work in a range of media. The quickest and most accurate was usually written text, and the video version was great fun but I am not sure that the complexities of staging and filming did not rather overshadow the reinforcement of the content, which was the primary purpose of the task. However, the total engagement of the teenage learners was unquestionable and so we see the careful balance that any teacher must strike between offering learners choice, an opportunity to work with rich media and the need to retain a focus on the content coverage. It is easy to see why, in an assessment-driven culture, the safe option is often seen to be the traditional one.

Learners in the one-to-one study referred to in Chapter 2 used the camera in their devices both spontaneously and under direction to capture still and moving images as records and made still and animated drawings. However, it was rare for these records to be discussed, evaluated or edited. With these rich texts in multiple formats, the potential to use them as tools to develop and hone thinking was not exploited. Photographic images and footage was created quite freely but there was little thought as to the relevance or quality of the product. When creating the 'mark' becomes as easy as pressing a button there is a risk that any thought as to purpose and meaning may be lost entirely. Even more so than with written texts, the need to be clear as to why the text is being created is vital and that has to start with the teacher's view of the role of text making in learning. The purpose of the text may then evolve but should be revisited during the task and always inform the final edit.

Who is the author?

The issue of changes and incorporations from other sources in students' writing, which do not leave a physical trace, is one that never ceases to arise in discussions about electronic texts in schools. As mentioned above, it is simple enough to keep versions of work as it develops when the text is digital, perhaps more so than with hard copy alone. But the mutability of digital texts always brings the shadow of the ease of 'copying' or simply downloading something and passing it off as one's own. Software tools make it easy for a teacher or assessor to check the source of a text or to compare two or more pieces of work to see if they are too similar. Knowing this will be done also focuses the mind of the students who are submitting work, especially for assessment.

A more interesting challenge arises when the final text is the result of an intentionally collaborative exercise where more than one person has legitimately contributed to the end product. Obviously judgements can be made on the end product as a whole, but which of the authors deserves how much of the credit? In professional contexts such collaborative work is the norm and there may be conventions as to who gets the credit. A novelist will have worked with an editor who may have made considerable contributions to the quality of the end product but only one name will appear on the cover. Similarly of the huge array of individuals who work together to make a feature film, the hierarchy of credit is established according to conventions and the end product is often regarded as the work of the director, as if he or she was the sole creative force, but the credits will list the very many people who have contributed to the whole creative process.

In a learning context such established hierarchies are not present and this is largely because we do not give accreditation to groups but to individuals. It is important to know who exactly did what and therefore whether or not they have passed the bar set to obtain the qualification in question at any stage in their education. This remains true from early years to post-graduate qualification.

Assessing literacy

The term literacy is used with various qualifiers such as visual, digital and even twenty-first century. In each sense it refers to an ability to understand information in a particular form or forms, and implies some skill in communicating meaning in that format too. In schools, however, and in local, regional and national comparisons of literacy, the scope is usually confined to the ability to code and decode written text. There can be little doubt that this is and will remain an important skill set; texting is more popular than phone calls, more novels are published per annum than ever before, most of the internet relies on a facility with text, and so on. New cultural forms rarely entirely replace one another, film did not replace theatre and TV did not replace film, even though the size of the audiences may change and the monopoly of a medium may be broken and we might now access all of these forms through a computer screen, given the popularity of webcasts of popular theatre performances.

The criteria by which we judge competence with written text remain somewhat fixed – a requirement for conventional spelling is back after a brief, more liberal period in the 1970s, even though the reasons we venerate correct spelling are not straightforward (see Spender, 1995, pp. 12–15). The creativity and innovation of electronic messaging is not tolerated in mainstream education. Yet the form and variety of texts we both encounter and can access tools to create has never been greater, and mass access has grown extremely rapidly.

In the early twentieth century photography was a rare, usually studio-based activity. Families who could afford it might have an image taken to record a special event. Now nearly everyone with a phone has a high-definition still and moving image camera in their pocket. Indeed there are concerns that we are all so busy snapping away on our phones we are less engaged with the real activity we seek to record. The result is that rather than one image that a few people have a treasured copy of, we have phones and websites full of images that anyone can see but possibly no-one does. In the mid-1960s television was very much a spectator sport, with one set in the living room of better-off families and viewing a widely shared cultural activity. Now we commonly have many sets in a house, and view TV through a computer. Appointment-to-view programming is becoming a quaint hangover. Although there are some who still watch at a given time when the content is first aired, the times when the majority of a nation sat and watched the same programme at the same time are almost certainly now confined to history. But more significantly, anyone with a camera – which is pretty much everyone with a phone – can shoot footage and post it to a public website. Content on sites such as YouTube posted by private individuals can attract viewing figures that rival TV of the past.

A 5-year-old coming to school will have had experience of decoding messages from a wide variety of sources in a wide variety of formats. An animated cartoon, the picture book that may contain the same characters, the cuddly toy of the same character, the computer game – these all convey different aspects of a complex web of narratives. But her decoding abilities go much further; she recognises the logo of the burger bar and it has meaning for her, she knows how to open her favourite game on her dad's phone, she knows how to switch on the computer, use a touchscreen and take part in video chats with her grandparents, she may even have her own tablet with learning games on it. None of these experiences will be exceptional or notable, they are all simply part of life in a rapidly growing proportion of the world. As Douglas Adams and Alan Kay have both pointed out, 'technology' is the stuff that is invented after you were born. So to refer to these activities as exceptional or attribute terms such as digital literacy to the common experiences of a contemporary child in the developed world seems rather redundant. And yet it is important since these competences do not develop spontaneously whatever the rhetoric and do not flourish into expertise to critique and create without guided experience. Schools and education policy makers have a responsibility to build appropriate experience of rich digital media into the curriculum. School leavers with general literacy that extends only to the ability to read and write written text are set to join the worryingly large and growing population of young adults without paid employment, and may well struggle to secure places in education beyond school.

Summary

International comparative studies suggest there is a problem with declining standards of literacy in the Anglophone world compared to other OECD member countries. This is one factor that has informed policy in the UK and US and led to a strong focus on teaching reading and writing and testing competence at regular intervals. Working with texts that are formed from media other than the written word is not as prominent in the curriculum and work in school with digital devices tends to focus on the operation of the technology – although strangely not mastery of the QWERTY keyboard.

Tools that allow us to work creatively with text, treating it as an expression of our thoughts and understanding to be manipulated and developed to reflect our learning, have been available in schools for decades. However, this is not how they have been widely used. This chapter examines the position of learners' authoring of texts in the context of the school curriculum, the potential of digital media to extent and transform the way we use text as a tool to think with and takes a look at why this opportunity is rarely used in schools.

References

Adams, A. (1990) The potential of Information Technology within the English Curriculum. *Journal of Computer Assisted Learning*, 6, pp. 232–8.

Bonnett, M. (1994) *Children's Thinking*. London: Cassell.

Crook, C. (1994) *Computers and the Collaborative Experience of Learning*. London: Routledge.

Crook, C., Harrison, C., Farrington-Flint, L., Tomás, C. and Underwood, J. (2010) *The Impact of Technology: Value-added Classroom Practice*. Coventry: Becta.

DES (1988) *Report of the Committee of Inquiry into the Teaching of English Language: The Kingman Report*. London: HMSO.

Egan, K. (1990) *Romantic Understanding: The Development of Rationality and Imagination, Ages 8–15*. London: Routledge.

Eraut, M. and Hoyles, C. (1988) Groupwork with computers. ESRC-InTER Occasional Paper, InTER/3/88, University of Lancaster. *Journal of Computer Assisted Learning*, 5(1), pp. 12–24.

Jessel, J. (1992) Do children really use the word processor as a thought processor? *Developing Information Technology in Teacher Education*, 5, pp. 23–32.

Kuhn, S. and Stannard, R. (1996) *IT in English; Review of Existing Literature*. Coventry: NCET.

Loveless, A. (1995) *The Role of IT: Practical Issues for Primary Teachers*. London: Cassell.

McMahon, H. (1990) Collaborating with computers. *Journal of Computer Assisted Learning*, 6, pp. 149–67.

OECD (2013a) *Skills Outlook First Results from the Survey of Adult Skills*. N.p.: OECD Publishing. http://dx.doi.org/10.1787/9789264204256-en.

OECD (2013b) *PISA 2012 Results in Focus*. www.oecd.org/pisa/keyfindings/pisa-2012-results-overview.pdf.

Peacock, G. (1993) Word-processors and collaborative writing, in Beynon, J. and Mackay, H. (eds) *Computers into Classrooms: More Questions than Answers*. London and Washington, DC: Falmer Press (pp. 92–7).

Peacock, M. and Breese, C. (1990) Pupils with portable writing, machines. *Educational Review*, 42(1), pp. 41–56.

Somekh, B., Lewin, C., Mavers, D., Fisher, T., Harrison, C. et al. (2002) *Impact 2 – Pupils' and Teachers' Perceptions of ICT in the Home, School and Community*. London: Becta/DfES.

Spender, D. (1995) *Nattering on the Net: Women, Power and Cyberspace*. Melbourne: Spinifex Press.

Stradling, B., Sims, D. and Jamison, J. (1994) *Portable Computers Pilot Evaluation Report*. Coventry: NCET.

Chapter 9

Manipulating data, seeing patterns

Drowning in information

Information has never been in such abundant supply. Whatever the question, the internet will produce some content that is at least vaguely relevant, if not the actual answer. Not only do we have access to an overabundance of information, the formats in which we see it are many and varied. The skill is not in collecting data, but in sorting, selecting, analysing and presenting them in ways that inform the original question. The information may be in the form of text, images or video, and many sources will have a numeric component. In many instances in school, learners also collect original data for themselves. Manipulating and understanding numeric data present particular challenges, which this chapter addresses. Luckily, as well as powerful search engines to locate information sources, we also have access to remarkable tools to help us manipulate what we find, the better to turn information into meaningful knowledge.

From information to understanding

Digital tools are available to manipulate and display data in many formats, each of which may offer insights into the relationships and patterns that exist. Once mastered, these tools can facilitate access to deeper understanding of the implications of data sets, which is an important step on the journey to convert information into personal knowledge. Some of the formats that attempt to reveal relationships between ideas are novel, such as 'word maps', 3D models, and so on, but others are tried and tested and remain powerful. One such is the use of forms of graph plotting. An exploration of the way graphs are treated in school, and the lack of deep learning that results, offers an interesting case study of how digital technologies can be used to revolutionise the way we approach learning and indeed what we regard as important to be learnt.

Graphing as an example of inauthentic learning

When dealing with numeric data, the first formats we meet are tables then graphs. Children meet these in pre-school and will continue to work with them in one form or another, at least until they leave formal education. Learning to plot graphs is usually set within the mathematics curriculum although subsequent production and interpretation can be found almost universally. Unlike some other school-based learning, graphs also have widespread relevance beyond the curriculum. Indeed, the Cartesian plot is such a universal format it is used throughout the media to represent relationships and change over time of everything from the likely outcome of an election to the cost of housing or time for a pain-relieving drug to act on a headache. This reflects the power of a graph to express the trends and patterns in the relationship between two or more varying factors, with a high degree of visual impact.

The widespread use of graphs might lead us to assume that they represent a method of communication that is widely shared and understood. However, research evidence suggests that even when children and young people have worked with graphs in many formats from an early age, the conventions of graphing remain poorly understood (APU reports, 1988, 1989; Swatton and Taylor, 1994; McFarlane et al., 1995; Friedler and McFarlane, 1997). By the age of 11 most children can make a good job of plotting a line graph, but only if they are told what range of values to use on each axis, which variable to put up the side and which along the bottom. This suggests that they can plot coordinates but have no real understanding of the conventions of graphing, how graphs work or why we use them. When it comes to interpreting graphs drawn by others, the situation also raises concerns. The majority of 11-year-olds are unable to describe and use patterns in graphs or to make predictions based on data shown (Taylor and Swatton, 1990). This skill deficit might not be too worrying if we could be confident that it was addressed in secondary education, but in fact the situation is little improved among 15- and 16-year-olds.

This level of understanding of graphs, an ability to perform an operation with little understanding of its meaning or relevance, represents a classic class of inauthentic learning. Learners produce graphs because they are told to, not because they are seeking understanding or insights that this form of data presentation can reveal. When researching this topic in a range of schools we asked learners why they plotted a graph as part of the science exercise they were pursuing and all the responses fell into one of two categories: because the teacher had told them to or because that was what they always did in science. This problem has been recognised for many decades. In 1989 Anita Straker, an innovative mathematics educator and researcher, recognised that learners spent a lot of time drawing and colouring in graphs rather than spending time looking at them to discover what they meant. Inspection reports in UK schools show that the situation has changed little in the intervening decades, despite access to powerful tools to automate the drawing of graphs so that time could in theory be devoted to the higher level thinking about the data rather than the manual operation. Moreover, there is a preference for drawing bar charts, as they are easier to plot and read, with no understanding of whether they are appropriate. In our research, line graphs were identified as in some way 'more accurate', but it is not always clear that this is said with understanding of what that means. In conversations that colleagues and I conducted with learners there was little evidence of understanding of the concepts of interpolation or extrapolation (we did not expect these terms to be used, nor did we use them ourselves). Few learners showed any awareness that they could use line graphs to estimate values between or beyond those they had actually plotted. These findings are particularly worrying given that these learners will have had frequent exposure to line and xy plots, in a wide variety of curriculum contexts. They will also meet graphs as a method used to influence their opinions on a whole range of issues in the world beyond school. Encouragingly, there is evidence that the judicial use of digital tools widely found in schools can help to remedy the obvious skill deficit that exists in children and young people's understanding of graphing, beginning early in the child's experience (McFarlane et al., 1995; Friedler and McFarlane, 1997).

The 'hierarchy' of graphing

To better understand the development of children's graphing I want to examine in some detail the early experiences children may have as part of the school curriculum, and the assumed hierarchy of ideas implicit in the progressive development of the graphing process. I will also look at the nature of data briefly, as this too is a key concept that underpins successful data interpretation. These ideas are crucial to an informed use of related digital tools for teaching the authentic use of graphing. I will then go on to suggest ways in which the use of these tools can help to make these concepts explicit to the learner.

As early as infant school, children may begin to use pictograms. An example might be a chart reflecting pet ownership. A picture of a dog, cat or any other animal represents each pet owned and these are assembled into columns to show how many people own each type. The completed chart, provided the pictures are all roughly the same size, shows at a glance which type of pet is most common, which is least popular, how many types of pet are owned, and so on. This type of chart is so popular in schools that a number of database and charting programs have been developed for schools that will allow the user to build pictograms easily and quickly, using pictures provided with the software or drawn by the teacher or children.

Once the basic experience of building a pictogram has been established, it can be reinforced by using the computer to carry out the labour-intensive activity of drawing and gluing. This is not to suggest that the concrete experience of working with physical assets is in any way superfluous or lacking in learning value. Indeed, that concrete stage may be a very important precursor for some children to the more abstract activity on the screen. But when the learning objective moves from learning about the protocols of constructing the pictogram to interpreting the data collected, the time-consuming manual operation can prove a distraction.

Time spent drawing a picture of the family pet may well cause a young child to forget entirely about the pictogram task. Moreover, if errors creep in during the execution, for example the dogs are all drawn at different sizes (as indeed the dogs themselves are likely to be) the resulting chart can be very misleading. It is very de-motivating and time-consuming to have to do it again and in reality this is unlikely to happen. So the class is left with a result from which it is very difficult to make the inferences of patterns and distribution that were the original intention of the activity.

It is easy to see how the abstraction of the bar chart evolves from the pictogram where each pet in the example above is replaced with a square of equal size. The line graph is then commonly introduced by drawing a line through the top of each bar on a bar chart. This seems like a simple and obvious way to make a link between a more concrete representation – the bar chart – and an otherwise somewhat abstract one – the line graph. However, discussions I have had with students in initial teacher training, and with some classroom teachers, confirm that there is often confusion about the type of data that it is legitimate to display in a bar chart or a scatter plot and those where a line graph is valid. Indeed teachers who are not trained in mathematics or science may be unaware of the significance of any difference between bar charts and different types of xy plot and treat them all as interchangeable. The xy graph may simply be regarded as a 'harder' or 'more accurate' kind of graph, reinforcing the confusions that can develop in the minds of the learners as reported above. Teachers and children may remain unaware of the difference between discrete, categoric data, which bar charts and scatter plots can represent, and continuous data for which line graphs are better suited.

Not all data are the same

For teachers of young children, or subjects where mathematics is not the primary focus, the distinction between discrete and continuous data may seem unnecessarily pedantic. However, it is important that teachers, in the process of structuring learning opportunities, understand the difference because otherwise the progression from bar charts to xy graphs can be very misleading for learners. As mentioned above, in order to progress to xy graphs, teachers often get children to join the tops of the bars in a bar chart. This may seem like a good way to move between the concrete and more abstract representations, and for some data types may be valid. But consider for a moment what the line drawn between two points on a graph actually represents. This line is not simply a way to emphasise the peaks and troughs, or make the shape more obvious, it implies that you can reasonably expect any coordinate on that line to be valid. It offers a way to work out what happens in between the points you plotted if the extra data had been collected or measured. In the case of the bar chart of pet ownership, where 5 children own cats and 10 own dogs, a reading from a line drawn between these two points would suggest that 7.5 children owned an animal that was half dog and half cat. Clearly this is nonsense; the pet data is discrete, each point in this case must be cat or dog and cannot be in between. Consequently a line graph of the pet data is not valid.

The language 'discrete' and 'continuous' may be problematic for some learners, especially the young, but the concept can be made accessible and then given its rightful label when appropriate. For example, consider a data-gathering exercise that looks at the size of children's feet. If this is measured in shoe sizes, each foot must fit into one size or another: shoes are only available in discrete sizes, you cannot buy a 5.67 or a 36.89, for example. These data therefore fit very well into a bar chart where each bar represents a particular shoe size, and its height is proportional to the number of people who take that shoe size. However, if the data are collected rather differently, and the actual length of each child's right foot is measured, the data will no longer fit into discrete categories. A human foot can take any value within quite a large range so these data are potentially continuous and can be more meaningfully plotted on an xy graph. The final tricky question is: should this be a line graph or a scatter plot? In other words, is it legitimate to join the points up? If you join up the points this is saying that it is reasonable to assume that any point anywhere on that line is likely to be valid. However, the class data only represent members of the class, and since it cannot be true that there will be someone in the class with every available length of right foot, it is not fair to suggest that this is true by joining up all the points.

Consider the two graphs, bar chart and scatter plot. The bar chart is useful for looking at distribution of shoe size in the class. You can see at a glance which is the smallest and the largest, which most common and rarest. The scatter plot may appear to offer more detail, but the features that stand out clearly on the bar chart will be harder to see. So in this case the bar chart of shoe size has much to recommend it, not because it is easier to draw or understand, but because it reveals information on frequency, that is how many times each size occurs in the class, more clearly than a scatter plot. If frequency data are what you want, the bar chart is the tool to use and the discrete data were the best kind to collect.

Other cases of inappropriate representation of data may be harder to detect. For example, suppose that children measure the temperature in the classroom every day at the same time. Temperature is clearly an example of a continuous variable. It can have any value in a given range, even if the school thermometer can only measure to the nearest degree. Also there is a second variable here, namely time, which is also continuous. So it seems reasonable for the data to be recorded on an xy plot. So far so good, but they may then join the points to make a line graph, since this looks like a good way to see if the temperature is generally rising or falling or staying the same as the weeks go by. However, the result may not fit what you know to be the actual events, which is not surprising when you consider what the line graph is implying about temperature changes between the points actually measured.

If the temperature at 10 a.m. yesterday was 12°C and today at the same time the temperature is 14°C, a line drawn between these two points implies that the temperature has risen steadily by 2 degrees over the intervening 24 hours, which is unlikely to be true. Joining up these two points is therefore not a valid graphing action; the line does not allow you to work out the temperature at any time in between your two measurements. This practice of interpolation is not one you might expect younger learners to name, but is quite a simple idea and can be posed to quite young children successfully. It allows them to make the choice between joining the points into a line graph or leaving them as a scatter plot, which in this case is a more valid way of displaying the data.

Admittedly this dot-joining convention is one that is openly broken in advertising, mass media and so on, even in reference books. Sometimes this is valid, where overall trends are more important than individual 'blips'. For example, the annual unemployment figures over a decade may show a trend that is more meaningful than the weekly or monthly variation so a line is drawn to emphasise the annual variation at the expense of the seasonal one. This is fine so long as everyone understands what is happening, and the generalisation is valid. However, to know if the generalisation is valid, you have to understand the basic rule in order to know when to apply it rigorously and when it is acceptable to bend it.

So to summarise, there are three types of graphs commonly used in schools: bar charts, line graphs and scatter plots. These are usually arranged hierarchically in the school syllabus, with bar charts coming before line graphs, and scatter plots given scant attention or even ignored since line graphs are used by default. (Pie charts are also used to display data, and are good for representing proportions. They are usually a special type of bar chart, where the fraction of a group falling into a given category is proportional to the size of a slice of the pie. Oddly these are often seen in primary schools as a simple format, although measuring angles accurately to make the pie chart is actually quite hard for young children.)

The perceived conceptual progression from bar charts to line graphs has as much to do with the difficulty associated with drawing them as with the concepts and conventions behind the patterns and relationships they reveal or disguise. Because bar charts are easier to draw and a short step on from the highly accessible pictogram, it is assumed they are easier to understand. Moreover, it is implied that they are a less sophisticated kind of graph, rather than a graph that does a different kind of job.

How can digital tools help?

The use of digital tools in the form of computer-based graphing packages can liberate children from the limitations of their motor skills, and free them to engage with ideas behind graphs at an early age. There may be an assumption, rarely articulated, that a child's cognitive development mirrors her motor development.

Research at Homerton College and elsewhere has shown that in the area of graphing this is not necessarily the case.

The variety of opportunities presented by the examples in the previous section, and the many other possibilities for data-handling, can stimulate the teacher to consider the importance of having clear learning objectives in terms of the outcomes before even beginning to collect data. If the learners are not yet experienced enough to set their own objectives, and plan a route to achieve them, the teacher must be clear about the possible outcomes of a data-handling exercise. Why are the data being collected, what questions do you want to address? Many teachers I meet have had very de-motivating experiences with digital data-handling activities. Because they are using the computer to handle information, they encourage children to collect and key in much larger volumes of data than they would consider using with paper-based recording and display methods. All too often they then find that they cannot perform the kinds of manipulation exercise they had in mind, because they have inappropriate data sets. The need to set clear objectives at the outset of a data-manipulation exercise is all too obvious. Whereas this element may be fudged when small amounts of data are collected and little time is devoted to a task, the bigger projects that the availability of digital tools may inspire mean that this is a crucial stage of the teacher's planning that cannot be overlooked. The success or failure of a data-collection and interpretation exercise will depend on being clear from the outset about the questions to be asked of the data. The appropriate data must then be gathered and entered into the right tool so that it can be manipulated, analysed and displayed in ways that illuminate the original questions and possibly throw up further interesting queries and relationships. The range of possibilities offered in a good data-handling package can stimulate teacher and learner alike to consider a range of options, try out a few ideas prior to embarking on the full task and build confidence more broadly with data interpretation.

Computer graphing

So how can the discussions and demonstrations of the different features of graphs and graphing outlined above be made accessible and explicit to learners? Clearly getting them to draw many graphs of different forms manually using the same set of data would be very time-consuming, and if the purpose was then to point out that some of them are inappropriate it would also be rather dispiriting. This is where the mutability of digital data comes into its own. There are many packages available in schools that will generate graphs of a variety of formats. Once tabulated data are entered, the data can be manipulated to produce a range of graph formats. Each one can be discussed and evaluated, and the merits and drawbacks of each can be explored. It will be important to differentiate between real and meaningful differences and those that are simply presentational detail. Time could be spent to little effect going through the different colour palettes, or fill patterns.

It will be important to shape the task so that the choice of final format is justified, possibly through group discussion and recording of the rationale for the choices made in the final report of the activity.

In an ideal package it is possible to configure the number and type of choices learners make about the way they display their data through the use of a template, for example. Many of the less complex packages designed for schools will default to a bar chart unless another selection is made, regardless of whether this is appropriate to the data set. This helps to reinforce the idea that bar charts are somehow 'easier' or the natural place to start. There can also be problems associated with professional spreadsheet packages, which largely originated as accounting packages. These assume that data are largely discrete and will produce bar charts of any data, which are largely meaningless. Even when xy plots can be plotted the process of doing so can be rather convoluted in comparison, again reinforcing the idea of a hierarchy of difficulty in the format itself. The selection of an appropriate package designed for the target age and stage is therefore important and there are many to choose from. The way in which graphs can be formatted is a good indication of how powerful the package will prove to be as a learning tool.

The advantage of these packages is not simply that they make quick work of the production of neat and varied graphs, potentially quicker and probably neater than those the learners themselves produce, although by the time the data are carefully keyed in the overall exercise may not be shorter. The power of the resulting graphs comes from the flexibility they allow. Once a learner has drawn a graph manually, even if there are major errors in it, it is unlikely that she will re-draw the entire thing, and if she does it is unlikely to be done joyfully. As a result she may only see one possible representation of her data. Serious errors, such as putting the wrong variable on an axis, or using an inappropriate range, are likely to be pre-empted by the teacher if spotted but there is no guarantee the learner will know why. Even if these decisions are made through a general questioning of the class, there is no guarantee that each learner will be equally thoughtful in their execution. The collected research available suggests that the traditional methods used to support learners in their use of graphing are largely unsuccessful in terms of developing true understanding of this set of tools to aid critical thinking. How much better then to produce a variety of graphs from a data set, quickly and easily in a graphing package, and to spend valuable lesson time with a teacher who can facilitate a discussion of which one to use and why, and what they reveal about the questions under investigation. The inappropriate plots can often provide the richest source of discussion, as when a package defaults to using the range of the data as the range on the y axis, which makes even the smallest change look significant. This opens a discussion about the importance of scales and of comparing like with like. Using only manually plotted graphs learners rarely get to have such discussions or to compare the appropriate and inappropriate in a positive way, and as a result rich learning opportunities may be lost.

There is an important caveat to be noted with respect to the powerful learning exercise of sketching graphs as a way of predicting the outcome of a data-collection or manipulation exercise. Digital graphing tools cannot do this as they rely on an actual data set to form any graph. Sketching is better done by hand or, if the result is to be included in a digital report, with a drawing package (although I would rather a hand-drawn sketch that gives total freedom of form and can be photographed or scanned for inclusion in a report). I once observed a very dispiriting lesson in a school where learners had access to personal devices. One pair of usually able boys decided to try and sketch a graph in Excel. Since they were usually competent and the teacher was wary of the computer as a graphing tool, they were left to waste an entire lesson failing to sketch the predicted graph. This should have been a two-minute precursor to a practical lesson. The example revealed that these students and their teacher had a tenuous grasp of digital graphing and, in the case of the teacher, an unhealthy level of respect for the technical competence of the students.

Data logging

Data-logging systems, where probes that measure a range of variables, temperature, sound, light and so on, are attached to a computer in such a way that the outputs they give can be read dynamically into a range of formats including graphs, have been available to schools for some decades. Various research projects have shown them to be very effective in supporting students to develop investigative skills, design experiments and interpret data more effectively. Research I undertook with colleagues working with learners across the school age range from as young as 7 years old looked at the ability of learners to build and interpret graphs before and after conducting simple science experiments. The control groups used thermometers and plotted their readings directly onto a pre-prepared chart, the experimental groups (in the same school and where possible with the same teacher) used the data-logging system with heat sensors and software, which produced a temperature vs. time line graph on the screen as readings were logged. Prior to the experiment both groups had had experience of the equipment they were to use and had measured temperature in various contexts, including going between hot and cold, and observed the effects on the graph shape of the changes they made. This early experience was very important, especially for the younger groups, as it introduced them to the idea of temperature as a measurable quantity. They also saw the effects on the shape of a graph of temperature over time during heating and cooling and when the temperature remained constant.

When the groups were reassessed after their experiences the groups using the probes and live graphs, that is data logging, showed significant development in their understanding of line graphs, and their ability to represent relationships between variables using this convention. This applied to questions using the contexts they had met, extrapolations from it and contexts that were very different. The children who had used conventional methods to record and display data, and had in fact spent far longer on the topic in most cases, showed no significant improvement in any of these skills. The exception was the group of 16-year-olds where their graphing skills did not improve in the control or the experimental groups, even though they started from a moderate base. However, it was noticeable that, unlike the other groups where the learners watched the graphs as they developed and discussed the patterns they saw, the older students, in the name of efficiency and encouraged by their teacher, left the computer to do the work while they wrote up their lab reports. As a result they missed out on a rich learning opportunity and illustrated very powerfully that the context of use is vital in determining the quality of the learning outcome, not just the potential of the tools being used.

In this project the learners who used data logging successfully were introduced to line graphs not as a Cartesian plot, where the ability to identify positions on a grid correctly was key to success and probably beyond the youngest groups in our study, but rather they were introduced to line graphs as a representation of the relationship between two variables, temperature and time. They saw a system they had direct sensory experience of, and the power to influence, depict change over time as a line graph. Their ability to read and interpret temperature/time graphs was greatly enhanced as a result even among 7- and 8-year-olds. It is particularly pertinent that their ability to sketch temperature/time graphs by hand to predict the behaviour of a novel system also improved.

The children using thermometers and entering readings onto a prepared grid, that is plotting as they went, showed no significant improvement in the same skill set, despite being taught by experienced teachers using exemplary methods but restricted to traditional equipment. Even though these children plotted as they collected readings, a process that might be thought to mimic the real-time plotting of the software, there was no evidence of any improvement in their understanding of graphs as a representation of changes in the variables they were studying, according to the test instruments used with both experimental and control groups. The younger learners had also had to spend longer learning to use the thermometers before they could begin to investigate.

The positive learning outcomes of the experimental groups showed some persistence. The children who had used the data logging were still better able to read, sketch and predict the shape of temperature/time graphs some weeks after the investigation. They were able to use the knowledge they had gained to work with graphs on paper, not just in the context of the data logging or on screen (Friedler and McFarlane, 1997). Although these experiences of data logging all took place in the context of a science investigation, there is evidence that the learners showed an ability to apply the knowledge they gained in alternative contexts. Moreover this evidence of new knowledge also persisted in post-tests some weeks after the original experience. This was further supported in informal visits to the classrooms up to a year later when the learners were still able to speak with understanding about the investigation and the graphs produced (Cole, 1993). This alone argues for the value of the experience, since the carryover of skills from one context to another is notoriously difficult to achieve and embedding understanding so that it persists is also challenging.

Although the equipment needed to carry out this work is relatively expensive it can be managed with few sets in a school as it is not necessary for each pupil to have access to a set or more than one class to be carrying out an investigation at the same time. In our research project, the teachers had free access to laptop computers and data-logging equipment; however, after some experimentation most teachers chose not to use more than four sets of equipment simultaneously. Groups of up to four students used the kit and any additional students worked on another activity until the equipment came available, possibly in a later lesson. One teacher chose to run the activity as one element of a circus of activities. These models allowed the teacher to give close supervision to the groups using the equipment without abandoning the rest of the class. As a result they could pose the key questions at the right moment to ensure the attention of the learners was directed to get the most from the activity. This model also created the opportunity for the first users to become mentors to the rest and pass on their knowledge of the equipment, reinforcing their own learning as a result while freeing up the teacher from supervising the solely operational aspects of the equipment. With appropriate timetabling a school could manage with a small number of sets of this equipment, an investment with a good return given the powerful learning it supports and the wider relevance of the data-manipulation elements of the activities.

Implications for the curriculum

In traditional curricula children are taught to draw graphs before they spend time interpreting them. Furthermore, they have little experience of discussions about why graphs are useful, and what different types of graphs have to offer when looking for patterns and relationships in data. In many curricula, even in science in secondary schools where you might expect to find it, the skills of interpretation – linking the events depicted and the symbolic representation of those events – are rarely explicitly taught. Rather, this appreciation is expected to develop by osmosis.

Traditional teaching methods are quite effective at teaching pupils the skills they need to create graphs manually, within very clearly set parameters – what to put on each axis for example – by the time they are 11, but even by 16 they are not always able to appreciate the power of a graph as a model of underlying relationships presented in this symbolic way.

The data collected by our research projects show that children can manage data-logging systems from as early as 7 and possibly younger, and this can be accommodated within the school curriculum. However, teachers need support to understand the power of these activities, how to operate the equipment and where to focus the learning. The result will be powerful learning outcomes that have proved intractable with traditional methods. Furthermore, our results suggest that introducing children to the line graph holistically, as a model of the relationship between changing variables, before introducing the manual skills of plotting, might be a way to bridge the conceptual gulf that otherwise develops. The problem persists in secondary students, where even able students may go through the motions of plotting graphs with little active thought. They cannot articulate why they use a particular form of graph, or why they use a graph at all. Perhaps shifting the activity away from the 'busy work' of drawing a graph – or as in our investigation, writing up the lab report while learners ignored the computer drawing the graph – to a focus on the phenomena under investigation and what the pattern emerging on the graph tells you about that process would better support higher-order thinking about the science under investigation.

Removing the need for manual plotting allows graphs to be introduced earlier and means they can be seen from the outset to be a valuable tool in representing and understanding the world rather than an inauthentic exercise in keeping learners occupied.

Summary

The use of graphs to display data and reveal patterns and relationships is widespread across the curriculum and in contexts beyond school such as popular media and advertising. Children meet graphs at an early age and will use them, predominantly in subjects such as mathematics and science, throughout their schooling. However, research has shown that the majority do not really understand the protocols of these powerful representations and, although they can plot graphs with guidance, they have an inauthentic grasp of this method of communication. Digital tools that not only create graphs but allow them to be manipulated or drawn in real time as physical events are observed can support a breakthrough in the development of understanding. This chapter draws on research studies with primary- and secondary-school students that show the impact on learning can be more widespread than the immediate context of the experiment under study, and persist over time.

References

APU (Assessment of Performance Unit) reports (1988) London: HMSO.

APU reports (1989) London: HMSO.

Cole, G. (1993) Getting down to graph roots. *Times Educational Supplement*, 26 March.

Friedler, Y. and McFarlane, A.E. (1997) Data logging with portable computers, a study of the impact on graphing skills in secondary pupils. *Journal of Computers in Mathematics and Science Teaching*, 16(4), pp. 527–50.

McFarlane, A.E., Friedler, Y., Warwick, P. and Chaplain, R. (1995) Developing an understanding of the meaning of line graphs in primary science investigations, using portable computers and data logging software. *Journal of Computers in Mathematics and Science Teaching*, 14(4), pp. 461–80.

Straker, A. (1989) *Children Using Computers*. Oxford: Basil Blackwood.

Swatton, P. and Taylor, R.M. (1994) Pupils' performance in graphical tasks and its relationship to the ability to handle variables. *British Educational Research Journal*, 20(2), pp. 227–45.

Taylor, R.M. and Swatton, P. (1990) *Assessment Matters No. 1 Graph Work in School Science*. London: HMSO.

Chapter 10

Looking to the horizon

Computers in schools

Since the advent of the personal computer in the 1970s there have been initiatives to put computers in schools. In the 40 years that followed the numbers of computers in education crept up, often in fits and bursts as one government scheme after another earmarked funds. In 2008 the global recession hit, government funding was constrained and for the first time the supply of computers to schools was stemmed. In fact, as the machines aged, the ratio of relevant, functioning computers to students in schools worsened. In the UK the dedicated agency for digital technology in schools was disbanded in 2007. Any budget for equipment and services has to come from the main school grant. At the same time personal and home ownership of all kinds of technology, but in particular smartphones and tablets, in all OECD countries has leapt. Internationally, education policy rhetoric continues to speak of twenty-first-century skills and familiarity with digital technologies generally as important objectives not least to ensure future economic growth.

Computer-based technologies have been hailed variously as a substitute for teachers, a way to teach as we had always done but more efficiently and as an agent for change that would revolutionise schools, teaching and learning. Research over the years has struggled to isolate and identify the exact impact of digital technologies on the learning of the children and young people who have been exposed to them. In the UK pilot projects of new technologies and research into the effects of what we have and how it is used to support learning have fallen back to small-scale studies following two major national research programmes, funded by the government research councils, into teaching and learning with technology and the development of technology-enhanced learning. Both of these produced some interesting outputs, but nothing that has informed systemic change.

Generally, research into the relationship between technology and learning finds that the effects are unpredictable, and the teacher is the key variable. In such research studies the impact on learning is invariably measured through standardised tests. The practice with technologies is so varied that even with the simplest implementation it is hard to know if research is comparing like with like. In their book *Enchancing the Art and Science of Teaching with Technology* Magaña and Marzano (2013) give a very comprehensive overview of the range of technologies that have a place in the classroom and some of the ways they can be used to achieve specific learning outcomes more efficiently.

In this book I have argued that it is the way a tool or resource is used that is key to the impact on learning. Meta-analysis is therefore challenging, as the precise mode of implementation is not always described. One of the most comprehensive attempts, which looked at many interventions, not just those using digital technology, is reported by John Hattie in his book *Visible Learning* (2009). Hattie attempted a synthesis of meta-analyses using effect size data, so they must have a numeric component to their data, which usually means test data. He found a medium effect size of 0.45 when technology was used to aid teacher instruction, but a small effect of 0.30 when the technology was used in an attempt to replace the teacher. Despite many years of investment and research into instructional technology, particularly in the US, as a replacement for teachers, and potentially a more effective one, the idea of computers as a substitute for teachers has now been largely discredited and fallen away in policy discourse. The focus is more towards use by teachers to increase impact and there is evidence from the meta-analysis that using technology to supplement traditional teaching does make a positive, if small, difference. However, large-scale reviews still show little regular use of technology in the classroom, with the majority of European classrooms using technology once a week, and therefore, unsurprisingly, little change in pedagogy as a result.

Such large-scale research tends to look at what is happening and not why, and it is all too easy to assume the low levels of computer use in the classroom are due to Luddite teachers who have little inclination to change their methods. However, this is too simplistic. Over the last 40 years the curriculum has been changed many times and in the UK the number of changes to external testing has been dizzying. Teachers have risen to the challenge and results in the formal assessment at 16+ and 18+ have steadily improved, although the international measures of basic skills are fairly static while other countries show improvements. This is not a profession stuck in a rut. Rather it is a profession that has met the challenge of change to what they teach on an annual basis. It seems teachers are very good at doing what curriculum and assessment policy asks of them. So the non-adoption of widespread use of digital technology may not be resistance to change but rather a combination of poor access to equipment and a perceived misfit between what the technology offers and the most effective way to prepare learners to perform well in high-stakes tests at the end of primary and secondary schooling.

Drivers of change in school practice

If technology is to act as an agent of change, then there has to be sufficient access for the frequency and duration of use to make a difference. The overall level of provision in most schools still makes this unlikely, hence the mean frequency of use in Europe is still struggling to rise above once a week. Even when the main model of use is collaborative within a small-group setting rather than a one-to-one model, the class needs open access to machines as and when needed, not in a pre-booked computer suite, which is still where most machines are in many schools. However, personal ownership of powerful devices among children and young people is significant and growing fast. If schools were committed to school-based use they could work with parents and carers to manage use in school and, perhaps more easily, encourage work on machines at home to support school learning. Indeed, aware that many children enjoy using devices and keen that this use should have some value in their development, parents are usually open to suggestions for activities to help with school work. In genuine hardship cases, schools could support access by loaning machines.

Having access to machines in school will not of itself bring about changes in pedagogic practice, as pilot after pilot has shown. The drivers for such change will inevitably come down to what wider society chooses to value as evidence of a 'good' education. Currently across the world this is primarily the results of tests, even though parents do generally look for more from a school, they also value test results. Without the right grades, the paths to the next stage in life, be it further education or work, will be restricted. The OECD has been working on the relationship between the results of its international comparative tests and the need for twenty-first-century skills. As a result, in 2013 they introduced a small-scale trial to test problem solving in a computer-based context, which was in itself done on a computer. The next step is a planned test of collaborative problem solving in a computer-based context. This follows pioneering work by an innovative research group in Santiago, Chile (Claro et al., 2012). It will be interesting to see the extent to which national governments respond to these developments in the PISA league tables, and if changes in statutory curricula result. It will also be interesting to see how the scores based on problem solving compare with those of basic skills in mathematics, science and reading. Devising an education experience that supports children and young people to develop both collaborative problem solving and basic skills seems to have proved difficult to date, and yet both are equally important components of functional literacy in a digital age.

It is interesting that the processes by which school performance are judged concentrate so fully on testing, and increasingly on computer-administered tests. Yet the skills at the heart of twenty-first-century learning are as much to do with interpersonal activity as they are to do with technology-based interactions or final output. The ability to work with others, analyse, synthesise and debate ideas are perhaps best assessed through interactions with other humans. Such teacher assessment is still used in higher education in some of the world's best universities and has been used in GCSE examination in living memory. Unfortunately, political trust in the professionalism of teachers is perhaps at an all-time low in English-speaking countries. As a result there is no evidence of plans to use such assessment to introduce an element of collaborative knowledge building skills in schools. The consequence is that, if this is to happen, we will have to wait for expensive and complicated computer-based tests to be developed and tested.

Meanwhile . . .

Not only are there concerns that compulsory education is not preparing young people for the world of work, the evidence of rising levels of unemployment among under-25s is all too apparent. Although this is in part due to the global economic downturn, it also reflects the lack of work-relevant experience among the young. Employers complain of a lack of basic skills, unfamiliarity with information technologies and lack of experience of team working and knowledge building.

Meanwhile, children and young people have growing and unsupervised access to digital technologies and the content and people this access connects them to. They are exposed to a range of content considered unsuitable for them, bullying behaviours and potential risk. For a majority is seems the creative possibilities are underexploited and their powers of discrimination regarding sources they find are poorly developed. The norms of behaviour are being set not only by what they experience in the real world but also by what they see and hear online. There are filters and other controls meant to protect them, but these are poorly understood by adults and ineffective when they are. Formal education does not seem to be stepping in to help them, while teachers comment on the poor concentration, information and writing skills, which they see as resulting from the exposure to short messaging and online activity. The most recent call in the UK is for improved relationship education to re-balance the view of sexual relationships formed by young people who look to the internet and porn for their education in the norms of physical relationships. Indeed, research into young people's exposure to porn makes the same recommendation.

Schools alone cannot solve all of society's ills, but they do have an important role to play in establishing norms of social interaction, particularly outside the home. Negotiating codes of behaviour in the face-to-face world and how to act in class are a normal part of school life. Extending this to how we behave online, and the relationship between what we find online and social norms, should not be impossible. But just as the analysis of popular broadcast and print media has been ridiculed as a lower order of intellectual activity, which reflects a 'dumbing down' of the school curriculum, are we also shying away from a serious appraisal of the online media our children spend their time with?

A tipping point?

For four decades, computers have been absorbed into schools, causing barely a ripple. The curriculum does usually contain a slot where everyone studies some aspect of computer use – although not how to touch type – but this rarely then flows across the rest of the subjects. Computer use can supplement traditional teaching; there is much research evidence to support this and detailed resources to show teachers how it can be achieved. Advocates of computer use have predicted revolution time and again, and time and again they have been proven wrong. Could it be that finally the step change in personal access to online resources and communications by children and young people using smartphones and tablets will be the factor that changes policy and therefore schools' attitudes to computer use? The needs of the workplace have not yet proven sufficiently pressing, but the adverse effects of untutored access by children and young people may finally tip the balance. As parents' concerns about the effects of constant connectivity without the skills to stay safe and make intelligent use of resources and communication become a campaigning cause for lobby groups and media, how will schools respond? Will policy makers modify the curriculum, and will those who design accreditation and inspect schools begin to demand evidence of a culture of informed and effective use of digital technologies by school-age learners?

In schools that are ahead of the curve in these matters, where preparing students to be effective, collaborative learners is taken seriously, head teachers in particular speak of taking risks. They are breaking away from traditional pedagogies that are better aligned to examination excellence, and using more innovative teaching approaches. They know that they will get little credit for this if the high-stakes test results do not continue to meet targets.

Final thoughts

It would seem that the context is set fair for a major change in schools, to finally embrace the calls for a pedagogy better aligned to a knowledge society, where education focuses on the skills needed to build understanding as well as familiarity with content. Personal ownership of powerful devices has leapt to the point where schools have only to provide for a minority in order to have one-to-one access as and when needed. The OECD is leading the way with recognition of the importance of collaborative problem solving in a computer-based context and we will soon be seeing comparative performance tables for 15-year-olds across the developed world. Concerns that children and young people are adrift on a sea of information without the skills and knowledge to make good use of digital technologies and stay safe online are leading to calls for schools to take a lead in the development of cyber-citizenship. Could it be that we will finally see a revolution in pedagogy, with a shift in emphasis towards more collaboration and problem-based learning using digital technologies to build and communicate evidence of knowledge and understanding, and where time with trained professional teachers is spent in discussion and argument about powerful ideas rather than predominantly transmission of content, and school leavers are better prepared for life in a knowledge society?

References

Claro, M., Preiss, D.D., San Martín, E., Jara, I., Hinostroza, J.E. et al. (2012) Assessment of 21st century ICT skills in Chile: Test design and results from high school level students. *Computers & Education*, 59, pp. 1042–53.

Hattie, J. (2009) *Visible Learning: A Synthesis of over 800 Meta-analyses Relating to Achievement*. New York: Routledge.

Magaña, S. and Marzano, R.J. (2013) *Enhancing the Art and Science of Teaching with Technology*. N.p.: Marzano Research Lab.

Index